FOUR HUNDRED
YEARS
on the Best Seller List

PHILIP C. STINE

ISBN: 0615620612
ISBN-13: 9780615620619

FOREWORD

In anticipation of the 400th anniversary of the King James Bible, the Eugene A. Nida Institute for Biblical Scholarship of the American Bible Society (ABS), working with the Society of Biblical Literature (SBL), organized two symposia, one in 2003 and the other in 2004, which were the occasion for scholars to present papers on the history and impact of the King James Bible. A number of those papers were subsequently published by the SBL in 2009 in *Translation That Openeth the Window: Reflections on the History and Legacy of the King James Bible* (TTOW), edited by David G. Burke.

Both the Nida Institute of the ABS and SBL saw the merits of producing other related publications including a narrative that drew on TTOW. This book is that narrative. Much of the information in this account is extracted from the twelve papers and the introduction of TTOW. I am grateful to acknowledge the articles by Alister McGrath, Benson Bobrick, Lynne Long, John R. Kohlenberger III, A. Kenneth Curtis, Barclay M. Newman and Charles Houser, Jack Lewis, Leonard J. Greenspoon, Cheryl J. Sanders, Lamin Sanneh, David Lyle Jeffrey, James R. White and David G. Burke. I depended significantly on their fine research and writing. Any errors are, of course, my own.

But to tell the whole story, there was a need for even more information than these twelve papers offered. For more material on developments in the English language, I referred to *The Cambridge Encyclopedia of the English Language* by David Crystal, to *Wide as the Waters: The Story of the English Bible and the Revolution*

It Inspired by Benson Bobrick, and also *The Bible Word Book: Concerning Obsolete or Archaic Words in the King James Version of the Bible* by Ronald Bridges and Luther A. Weigle.

For more examples of literature that had been influenced by the King James Bible, I read with delight *Chapters into Verse: A Selection of Poetry in English Inspired by the Bible from Genesis through Revelation* edited by Robert Atwan and Laurance Wieder. Robert Alter's *Pen of Iron: American Prose and the King James Bible* stimulated my thinking as well. Three more sources on the history of the writing, publishing and influence of the King James Bible were *God's Secretaries: The Making of the King James Bible* by Adam Nicolson; *A History of Bible Translation and the North American Contribution* by Harry M. Orlinsky and Robert G. Bratcher; and *In The Beginning: The Story of the King James Bible and How It Changed a Nation, a Language, and a Culture* by Alister McGrath. All of these give much more detail and description of the topics they deal with than is possible here. Of course, the other side of that is that none presents the wider range of material that this book covers.

"The Translators to the Reader," the original preface of the 1611 editions of the King James Bible, is an important part of the story. Erroll F. Rhodes and Liana Lupas edited this material, and I am grateful to them and the American Bible Society for publishing this preface and making it accessible.

I received valuable comments from Charles Houser and Philip Towner of the Nida Institute, from David Burke, former director of the Nida Institute, and from Kent Harold Richards and Bob Buller of the Society of Biblical Literature. It would have been very difficult to bring all this together without their clear direction and assistance.

CHAPTER ONE

HOW IT CAME ABOUT

For four hundred years one English translation of the Bible has dominated every other translation. It has been the principal Bible for millions of English speaking Christians. This translation, published in 1611, is widely known as the King James Bible, after the king of England who commissioned it. Despite the abundance of modern translations, the King James Version is still for many the Bible they turn to for inspiration, solace and guidance. This Bible has influenced the development of the English language, English oratory and English literature worldwide, and is a central artifact in the culture of the English speaking world. Politicians are sworn into office with their hands on this Bible, and they quote from it in their speeches, expecting their audience to recognize the references. Court witnesses place their hands on it as they swear to tell the truth. Television quiz shows pose questions based on this Bible. Poets and writers have been inspired by it, and it has shaped the theology of much of the Christian church. Its influence has extended well beyond native English speakers, as translators in hundreds of languages have been guided by the text and language of this Bible.

POLITICS AND TRANSLATION

How did this all come about? How did the King James Bible come to be? How was the translation process started? Who were the people who created it? What issues did they face? How did they go about producing the translation? How was it received? Why is it still so often given as gifts to children for birthdays or at the time of their confirmation? What is so special about it? In short, what led to the production of this monument of the English language?

The full answer to these questions is as fascinating as it is complex, involving the intricate politics during the period of the Tudor and Jacobean rulers in England, the hopes and fears of English monarchs and would-be archbishops, and the surge of confidence and pride in England and its national language under Elizabeth I.

The Tudors were a family who ruled England and its realms from 1485 – 1603. The dynasty began with Henry Tudor and ended with the death of Elizabeth I. "Jacobean" refers to a period in English and Scottish history that coincides with the reign of King James I (1603 – 1625) who was also James VI of Scotland.

The story begins with the death of Elizabeth I in 1603. She had transformed the fortunes of the English people and the English language. During her reign, nevertheless, there had been serious religious tensions between Anglicans and Puritans that could have torn England apart had they been handled badly. The Roman Catholics for their part were bitter that they were deprived of many of their rights. Under Elizabeth, the tensions had been contained, in no small part as a result of her charisma and authority. But her death after forty-three years on the throne left a power vacuum, and it was inevitable that her successor would face enormous difficulties. Unless religious peace could be secured quickly, there was a real risk of England fragmenting and drifting into civil war.

Under Henry VIII who reigned from 1509 to 1547, the English church separated from the Roman Catholic Church. However, many English religious leaders known as Puritans felt that the English religious leaders known as Puritans felt that the Anglican Church retained too many of the rituals and ceremonies of the Catholic Church, as well as customs such as priests wearing surplices and the prominence given to the emblem of the cross. These Puritans wanted to complete the Reformation by eliminating these practices.

JAMES AND THE PURITANS

Elizabeth's successor was James VI of Scotland who became James I when he took the English crown. Many regarded him as having Puritan sympathies, and news of his succession to the English throne alarmed the English religious establishment and gave new hope to the Puritans. Might this new king give them privileges and rights that Elizabeth had denied them? While journeying south from Scotland to be crowned, James was met by a Puritan delegation and presented with the Millenary Petition, so called because it was said to have been signed by more than one thousand ministers of the Church of England. The authors had, they declared, served their church faithfully, despite their serious misgivings concerning its practices; the time had come now for change. James was clearly expected to deliver changes if he wished to retain the support of his more radical subjects.

But it was not entirely correct that James was sympathetic to Puritanism. He was a forceful believer in the doctrine of the divine right of kings, something the Puritans found at best puzzling and at worst downright offensive. But Anglicans found that their emphasis on the central religious and political role of the monarch in the life of both church and state offered them a way to ingratiate themselves with James and temper his alleged Puritan leanings.

The divine right of kings is a political and religious doctrine that asserts that a monarch derives his right to rule directly from the will of God. He is not subject to the will of his people or the aristocracy, not even to the church. The doctrine implies that any attempt to depose the king or to restrict his powers runs contrary to the will of God and could be considered heresy.

James wanted unity and stability in his church and state. Aware of the importance of maintaining religious peace, James decided to buy time. On October 24, 1603, he issued a proclamation that he was convening a conference in January of the following year at the palace of Hampton Court, a magnificent estate about fifteen miles southwest of London, to be attended by himself, his private advisors known as the Privy Council, and various "bishops and other learned men" to deal with religious issues. Leading figures of the religious establishment, as well as a smaller group of Puritan leaders, would participate. This conference was to prove of decisive importance in bringing the King James Bible into existence.

The Conference at Hampton Court

The participants met in the Privy Chamber of the palace. They included the king, the Privy Council of advisors, and nine bishops and deans. The bishops included the Archbishop of Canterbury, John Whitgift, and the Bishop of London, Richard Bancroft, who succeeded Whitgift as Archbishop of Canterbury in 1604. Also present were four Puritan representatives, John Reynolds, head of Corpus Christi College, Oxford; Laurence Chaderton, a noted preacher and master of Emanuel College, Cambridge, a Puritan stronghold; John Knewstubs, rector of Cockfield in Suffolk; and Thomas Sparks, a preacher. On the first day of the conference these Puritans were not allowed to attend. But they were invited to join the meeting on the second day.

During the conference James was able to resist without undue difficulty most of the Puritan demands for reform; however, he clearly felt the need to make at least some conciliatory gesture, even if it were more token than real. His opportunity came when John Reynolds suggested that a new translation of the Bible be authorized. There is some evidence that this proposal may have been an attempt to secure official recognition of the Geneva Bible of 1560 along with the Bishops' Bible which Puritans disliked but which was the only translation authorized to be read in church. James saw his opportunity to offer the Puritans a small concession. Against the advice of senior Anglicans, he declared the commissioning of a new Bible translation. Work on it would begin immediately.

The two most widely used Bibles in England at that time were the Geneva Bible and the Bishops' Bible. The Geneva Bible had been translated by some English Protestants who had fled to Switzerland to avoid persecution during the time of the Catholic queen Mary I. It was published first in 1560 in Geneva, although not printed in England until 1575. It had extensive notes which were Calvinist and Protestant in nature. The Bishops' Bible was produced as a response to this. Based on an earlier translation known as the Great Bible, so named for its size, it had been prepared by fourteen bishops, but most biblical scholars did not consider it a very good translation. Although it had official recognition and was used in the churches, it never achieved the popularity of the Geneva Bible which was printed privately. Whatever Reynolds may have hoped for, he seems to have been presented with just what he did not want, namely a translation to be revised by bishops, approved by the Privy Council, and this to be the only translation that could be read in church. The Geneva Bible would be limited to the privacy of people's homes and could not be used for public preaching.

We may surmise that James liked the idea of a new translation. He despised the Geneva Bible. It wasn't so much the quality of this translation that bothered him but he found the marginal notes that contained commentary and interpretation subversive. For example, in Exodus 1.19 the Hebrew midwives lie to Pharaoh to protect the Hebrew babies. The Geneva Bible note suggests that their disobedience was lawful, even though deception was evil. James could not tolerate justifying disobeying a monarch. To his mind, that was sedition.

ORGANIZING THE PROJECT

James divided the text of the Bible into six sections and assigned each to a "company," allocating eight people to each, plus a director so that the total number of translators in the six companies was to total fifty-four. Two of the companies were assigned to meet at Westminster, two at Oxford University, and two at Cambridge University. Three companies were assigned the Old Testament, and two, the New Testament. The sixth company was entrusted with the apocryphal works. When the companies had completed their tasks, two delegates from each would meet together to review and revise the entire work. Finally, the bishops of Winchester and Gloucester would apply the finishing touches. Richard Bancroft, who later became Archbishop of Canterbury, reserved for himself the privilege of making revisions to the final draft.

The Apocrypha, which means "hidden", refers to a number of books that many Christians considered useful but not divinely inspired. In some traditions, including the Roman Catholic Church, they have been included in the canon, that is, they are part of Scripture. Others, including most contemporary Protestants, do not consider them Scripture. They were included in the King James Bible.

> The Archbishop of Canterbury is the chief bishop
> and principal leader of the Church of England. Today
> he is the symbolic head of the worldwide Anglican
> Communion. Since the Church of England was the
> official state church, at that time the Archbishop of
> Canterbury was appointed by the monarch.

The use of the terms "company" and "director" were suggestive of commercial organizations. Such an enterprise distinguished this project from most other translations which were done either by one person or by a single committee. For example, in Germany, Martin Luther translated the New Testament by himself, and had only six collaborators for the Old Testament. There was no formal structure or review process. William Tyndale translated the New Testament and most of the Old Testament into English working alone. His work was completed by Myles Coverdale, who translated the rest of the Old Testament and most of the Apocrypha, and John Rogers, who translated one book of the Apocrypha from a French translation and then had the whole Bible published under the assumed name of Thomas Matthew, hence the name "Matthew's Bible." When in 1535 Coverdale put his work and Tyndale's and Rogers's materials together, the result was essentially the first complete Bible to be printed in English. The Matthew's Bible appeared in 1537, two years later.

The organization of the King James translators would mean that individual preferences and interpretations would not survive the review process. It was a managed process. Bancroft was determined to ensure that the translation process would be judiciously guided and the freedom of the translators limited. The translators were instructed to follow strict rules of translation, drawn up by Bancroft and approved by James, designed to minimize the risk of producing a Bible that might give added credibility to Puritanism, Presbyterianism, or Roman Catholicism. The rules gave precise directions on how certain potentially sensitive words were to be translated, as well as an insistence that earlier translations, including that of William Tyndale, should be used as the basis of the new translation, except where scholarly accuracy demanded deviation from its form.

Instructions

There were fifteen separate instructions given to the translators. The first stated that the Bishops' Bible was to be the base for the translation, altered only as required for accuracy. The Bishops' Bible was not considered as good a translation as the Geneva Bible, but since it was the official Bible, it had to be respected. In the end, however, it contributed no more than eight per cent of the phraseology to the King James Version.

The translators drew on a number of other translations, perhaps none more than Tyndale's. But, of course, they also found their own ways to express the meaning.

The second instruction insisted on using the names that were commonly used for most biblical figures, not the translation of those names. Thus, for example, "Isaac" and "Timothy" would be used, not "He Laughs" and "Fear God," the literal meaning of their names. However, the translators did not follow this rule completely as they paid attention to the forms in the original text although these were not completely consistent throughout the Bible. So the prophet "Isaiah" also appears as "Esai" in 2 Kings 19.2 and "Esaias" in the New Testament.

Both of these instructions could be seen as denying the preferences of many Puritans. Similarly, the third instruction insisted on ecclesiastical vocabulary rather than on usage that had arisen in the Reformation. So "church" would be used, not "congregation" as Tyndale had introduced in his translation, and "priest" was to be preferred over "elder." Such changes retained the central authority of the church rather than placing it with the individual believer.

The instructions also valued the inherited interpretation of ancient church authorities over attempts to find authentic interpretation in the ancient texts. For many complex passages of Scripture the Church of England followed the interpretation and understanding of ancient church authorities such as St. Jerome, St. John Chrysostom, St. Augustine and Origen. Several of the King James translators had studied these authorities in some depth. In this the English Church differed from the reformed churches in Europe which broke more completely with traditional church interpretation. The King James Bible was to reflect this reliance on tradition.

Jerome (347 – 420) is known for his translation of the Bible into Latin and for his biblical commentaries. St. John Chrysostom (347 – 407) was the Archbishop of Constantinople. He was known for the elegance of his preaching and oratory, and after his death was given the nickname *chrysostomos* which means "golden mouthed." He is also known as a theologian and liturgist. St. Augustine (354 – 430) was born in what is present day Algeria. He is considered one of the most important figures in the development of Western Christianity. Augustine developed the concept of the Church as a spiritual City of God distinct from the material Earthly City. His thought profoundly influenced the medieval worldview. Origen (185 – 254) was an early Christian scholar from Egypt.

The translators were also instructed to retain the division of chapters and verses commonly used at that time. The thrust of these two instructions was to insist on continuity with church tradition and usage.

The instructions also called for there to be no notes in the Bible except to explain "the Hebrew or Greek Words, which cannot without some circumlocution, so briefly and fitly be expressed in the text." These notes were to be put in the margins so that the Bible was seen as one text. This rule was actually very significant. First, it indicated that although the first instruction stated that the Bishops' Bible would be the base, in fact the translators would base their work on the Greek and Hebrew texts, the original languages. This differed from Roman Catholic practice which took the Latin Vulgate translation as the standard. Secondly, it meant that there could be no theological or doctrinal slant added to the translation.

In practice, these notes do more than explain difficult words. Many of the Greek and Hebrew words in the Bible can have more than one meaning. The translators had to decide which was the most likely in a particular verse. In other places, there were variants in the Greek and Hebrew texts they had, and the translators had to make a decision of which to follow. In these kinds of situations, when the translators were not sure of their decision they gave the alternate meaning in a note.

In the preface of this Bible, the translators state that they did not rush their work, but gave themselves all the time necessary to study problems they faced and to make the best decision possible. They also state,

> *Nor did we hesitate to consult the work of translators or commentators, whether [ancient ones] in Aramaic, Hebrew, Syriac, Greek, or Latin, or [modern ones] in Spanish, French, Italian, or German.*

They do not list these commentaries and translations, but this statement shows that they were attempting to make use of the best contemporary and ancient scholarship. They also expressed complete willingness to correct and revise their drafts:

> *We did not refuse to revise what we had done, and to bring back to the anvil what we had once hammered.*

In this way they assured readers that this translation was as reliable as they could make it.

Other instructions outlined the procedures for the drafting, exchanging of manuscripts and the approval process. By the time they were in final form, the texts would have gone through at least four reviewing processes. In this way there was very tight control of the uniformity and quality of the final product.

Each man (for all were men) in each company would translate the same passages. When the company met, they would agree on a draft and then send that to the other companies. The instructions stated that the king was quite insistent on this point. These other companies would note places where they disagreed or had recommendations. Particular problems could be referred to experts who were not part of the drafting process. There is very little evidence that this actually happened. William Eyre, one of the translators, wrote to the Archbishop of Armagh in Ireland, James Ussher, on December 5, 1608 about progress in the work and referred to a copy of some of the translation that had been loaned to "D. Daniel for his use." Some scholars think that this is evidence that the instruction to refer questions to other experts was, in fact, carried out.

At the point when the companies had revised their drafts, the bishops were asked to seek input from their clergy and to send their comments to the companies either at Westminster, Cambridge, or Oxford. The directors there were the Deans of Westminster and Chester Cathedrals and the king's professors in Hebrew or Greek at the two universities.

One manuscript named Lambeth MS 98 appears to be a master copy held by the Westminster Company for annotating as they received suggestions and recommendations.

At Cambridge and Oxford Universities, there were certain distinguished scholars who had been appointed to their positions by the monarch. They are also known as regius professors.

The translators were allowed to use Tyndale's, Matthew's, Coverdale's, Whitchurch's and the Geneva translations when they were closer to the biblical text than the Bishops' Bible. They could in this way build on the scholarship of the previous eighty years. Although the translators undoubtedly had access to the Roman Catholic translation known as the Douai-Rheims which was nearing completion at that time, it is not listed as one they referred to.

This translation was based on the Latin Vulgate translation. A number of English Roman Catholics had taken refuge in Douai, and later in Rheims, in France. The New Testament was published in 1582. The Old Testament was published in two stages in 1609 and 1610.

EARLIER TRANSLATIONS

It is interesting to note that Tyndale's work had been considered seditious in his day. Both he and John Rogers were burned at the stake for their efforts to bring the Bible to ordinary people in their language. But shortly after Tyndale's martyrdom in 1536, Myles Coverdale who had completed most of the Old Testament of Tyndale's Bible, was commissioned by Sir Thomas Cranmer at the request of Henry VIII to prepare a Bible to be placed in all the churches. Because of the size of the pages it was known as the Great Bible when it appeared in 1539. Another name for it was the Chained Bible since the instructions were that it was to be chained in some convenient location in each church, chained, presumably, so it could only be read in church and not taken for private use. It was initially printed in France, but subsequently in England by Edward Whitchurch, hence the name Whitchurch's Bible. It was also known as "the Treacle Bible" because of the rather unusual way that Coverdale translated Jeremiah 8:22 "treacle in Gilead" instead of the more common "balm in Gilead."

Matthew's, Coverdale's and Whitchurch's Bibles were very dependent on Tyndale's translation. Many of the best known renderings in the King James Bible therefore had their origin in Tyndale. The differences came from the clear instructions they were following on key ecclesiastical vocabulary, as we noted above, and on the access they had to biblical source texts that Tyndale had not had.

The translators took very seriously the instruction to refer to these other translations. They were very conscious of the fact they were building on the work of others in what was essentially a corporate endeavor. The preface to the Bible, titled "The Translators to the Reader," made this very clear:

> Truly good Christian Reader, we never thought from the beginning that we should need to make a new translation, or even to make of a bad one a good one . . . but to make a good one better, or out of many good ones to make one principal good one.

Rather than trying to denigrate the work of their predecessors, they felt they were simply continuing in their tradition, using the tools and texts that were not necessarily available earlier.

FOLLOWING THE HEBREW AND GREEK

The first of Bancroft's instructions directed the translators to base their work on the Bishops' Bible. In line with this, in the preface the translators state that their intention was not to make a new translation. And yet the translators also state clearly that they worked from the Hebrew text for the Old Testament and the Greek text for the New Testament. Referring to Zechariah 4.12, they write:

> *These are the two golden pipes, or channels, through which the olive branches empty themselves into the gold. St. Augustine calls them precedent, or original, languages; St. Jerome calls them fountains. . . . These languages therefore (that is, the Scriptures in those languages) were what we based our translation on, because it was in these languages that God was pleased to speak to his Church through his Prophets and Apostles.*

Most of the writings of the Old Testament were written in Hebrew. But after Alexander the Great (356 – 323 BCE) conquered much of the Middle East, Greek became the language of commerce and government throughout the region. As the Jews were scattered throughout that part of the world, many of them did not have access to the Hebrew Scriptures. In the Greco-Roman era, they were more likely to be literate in Greek than in Hebrew. Between the third and first centuries BCE, various scholars translated these scriptures into Greek to make them more accessible. These works came to be known as the Septuagint, the translation of the seventy, because of the legend that they had been done by seventy-two translators in seventy-two days. It was certainly this Greek translation of the Old Testament that the Gospel writers most often quoted, not the Hebrew.

After the Roman emperor Constantine's conversion around 313 CE, when Christianity would become the official religion of the Roman Empire, Latin became the most used language not only of government and trade but of the western church, based in Rome. Very early, different scholars began to translate various books of the Bible into Latin. In 382 CE, Pope Damasus I commissioned Jerome, a priest and scholar from Illyria who was studying in Rome, to revise an old Latin translation of the Gospels. Jerome, who lived from approximately 347 to 420, continued for the rest of his life to translate and revise the Old

Testament, working from both the Hebrew and the Septuagint versions. Although he is known to have prepared other texts from the New Testament besides the Gospels, a number of New Testament books were translated by other scholars. By the thirteenth century, the resulting Bible was known as the *version vulgata*, which means "the commonly used translation," and it became the official Latin version of the Roman Catholic Church after the Council of Trent which met from 1545 to 1563. After Johannes Gutenberg developed a printing press with movable type around 1449, one of his first publications was an edition of the Vulgate Bible. This appeared in 1454 or 1455.

There was a series of twenty-five sessions that met during these years, most in Trent in present-day Italy, and some in Bologna, also in Italy. Considered one of the most important councils of the Roman Catholic Church, the church leaders condemned what they called the heresies of the Protestants, but in so doing the council also clarified church positions on salvation, sacraments and the canon of the Bible. The total effect brought about what became known as a Counter-Reformation.

TECHNOLOGY AND ACCESSIBILITY

This was not the first time that new technology made the Bible more widely accessible than previously. The ancient Hebrew manuscripts were generally written on scrolls which were usually some type of animal skins that were then rolled up. To read them, it was necessary to unroll them to find the passage that the reader might be searching for. But quite early, by at least 400 CE, the scribes who copied the writings of the New Testament authors used a new technology called the codex. Separate pages were bound together and often given a cover, very much like modern books. This made it easier to transport the texts, and it was also easier for readers to find the places in the texts that they wanted to read. Thus the codex made New Testament writings far more accessible than would have been possible with scrolls.

In the seventeenth century, Latin was still the language of scholars and the universities, and all of the King James translators would surely have been able to read the Vulgate, which was one of the major texts they consulted in their work. But rather than base their work on the Latin of the Vulgate, they took the Hebrew as their base for the Old Testament and Greek for the New, a practice which most Protestant translators still follow.

Erasmus and the Textus Receptus

The authors of the New Testament books wrote in Greek. Before the introduction of printing, the only way to circulate copies of these books was to make hand-written copies of other hand-written copies. Over the centuries, many textual variations were introduced either by circumstance such as when one scribe misheard what was being dictated by another, or purposefully, for example in order to better explain something the scribe did not understand. After Gutenberg, a Dutch scholar named Desiderius Erasmus gathered up the best manuscripts he could find of the various New Testament books and prepared a Greek New Testament that was published in 1516 by the Swiss publisher Froben. This was the first printed Greek New Testament, and with some editing and revision by other scholars and publishers, continued to be used widely well into the nineteenth century. It came to be known as the *Textus Receptus*, which means "Received Text." It was not called this because of any official church action, but simply because most New Testament scholars based their work on it.

None of the Greek texts that Erasmus had at his disposal was older than the tenth century. During its first hundred years, Erasmus's text was revised by others as they compared different manuscripts. One of the more prominent of these revisers was the Parisian printer Robert Estienne, known as Stephanus, who published several editions of the Greek New Testament, all of which were based on Erasmus but which contained notes that commented on the differences in some of the manuscripts used. In 1551 Stephanus published the first Bible that was divided into verses. The most significant reviser of this period was Theodore Beza (1519 – 1605), the French Protestant theologian and biblical scholar who had replaced Calvin in Geneva after his death. He released nine different editions between 1565 and 1604. Despite the fact that Beza's theology was certainly too Calvinist for the liking of James or most of the translators, the King James translators made use of Beza's editions in their work since these were the best editions available to them. However, they certainly had a number of the different editions of the Greek to refer to.

NEW DISCOVERIES

In the nineteenth and twentieth centuries, a number of much older, less corrupt manuscripts and papyri were found and studied. This made it possible for scholars to correct some of the passages in the Greek New Testament and the translations based on them such as the King James Bible. Some of the best of these manuscripts date to as early as the fourth century, making them at least six hundred years to a thousand years older (and closer to the originals) than any that were available to Erasmus, and therefore to the King James translators. One example is found in Matthew 17.21. In this verse, Jesus is speaking of casting out demons, and says in the King James Version, "Howbeit, this kind goeth not out but by prayer and fasting." This verse may well have been added by eighth century ascetic monks. It does not appear in older manuscripts, and most modern translations omit the whole verse.

Differences like this do not necessarily mean that the King James Bible was unreliable. To a very significant degree, the changes and variations in the text did not seriously affect any major teaching of the Christian faith, although even today practices and beliefs in some churches are based on texts that did not occur in the older manuscripts, or differed from them. An example is the Lord's Prayer in Matthew 6.9-13. The King James Version, based on the Textus Receptus, includes an ending "For thine is the kingdom, the power, and the glory, for ever. Amen." But since this ending is not found in older manuscripts, most later translations, for example the Revised Standard Version or the Good News Bible, do not include it. They do, however, place it in a footnote where they explain that some ancient authorities include some form of this ending. Quite possibly it was added to later texts because of its constant use in worship.

Another example comes from the end of the Gospel of Mark. The oldest manuscripts end abruptly at 16.8 with the words, "for they were afraid." However, since this ending seemed too negative to many readers, over the centuries other ancient authorities added various other endings, and these were included in the Greek texts that the King James translators followed. One, printed in the King James Version as verses 14 to 18, includes the statement that believers "shall take up serpents; and if they drink any deadly thing, it shall not hurt them." On the basis of the promises of this passage some churches still practice handling venomous snakes as a demonstration of their faith. Those translations that do not include this passage in the text do not give any scriptural support to this belief and practice. Most of these translations explain in a footnote that the oldest New Testament manuscripts do not give support to these later additions.

THE WORK PROCEEDS

Very little material evidence or documentation from the time of the translation remains. One document appears to be a master copy held by the Westminster Company for annotating as they received suggestions and recommendations. It is known as Lambeth Palace Manuscript 98. (Lambeth Palace in London is now the home and offices of the Archbishop of Canterbury.)

There is a single complete annotated copy of the Bishops' Bible dated 1602 in the Bodleian Library at Oxford University. It is thought that it is one copy of an edition that was printed especially for the King James translators to use.

One member of the Second Cambridge Company, the company charged with translating the Apocrypha, was John Bois (1560 – 1643) (also spelled "Boys"). Anthony Walker, a contemporary, wrote a biographical sketch of Bois in which he refers to notes that Bois kept of the proceedings of the translation. A corrected copy of these notes was discovered in the library of Corpus Christi College, Oxford, and published in 1966. The notes indicate that the translators discussed the drafts vigorously. Apparently, however, few of the recommended changes that Bois noted appear in the final text of the King James Bible.

The fifty-four translators specified by James never met. Different lists of the names of the translators show forty-seven or fifty-one names. It may well be that early deaths of some of the translators led to a smaller number of translators than what King James originally envisioned. Or these differences could be accounted for by Bancroft's fifteenth rule which allowed for "three or four" additional people as needed to be allocated to the translation companies. Perhaps fifty or fifty-one people were named initially with the assumption that three or four others would be called on as necessary.

The translation work was underway in earnest by late 1604. By 1610, it was largely finished. After the six companies of translators had completed their assignments, a final scrutinizing committee examined their translations for consistency and accuracy. The work was then passed on to the king's printer, Robert Barker for typesetting and printing.

One scholar's Recollection: In 1949 I graduated from seminary and was installed as pastor in a historic rural congregation in the Valley of Virginia. The congregation included families in their third and fourth generation of membership who claimed ancestral memories of the settlement of the Valley by Presbyterians from Scotland. The minister who was my predecessor had served for some twenty-four years. For that Church to call a young man fresh out of seminary was at least in part a response to the hopeful changes brought about by the conclusion of the Second World War.

My Seminary education had emphasized biblical study. When the New Testament of the Revised Standard Version was published in 1946 it became the constant companion of all the students. I carried an already well used copy of it with me, confident that its introduction would be a centerpiece of my ministry.

On my first visit to the pulpit I found a large, lovely, and apparently quite old Bible open as if waiting to be read. The pages exhibited signs of years of regular use, though still in quite good condition. Inscriptions on its presentation page indicated that it had been given in the late nineteenth century by the ancestors of one of the current families in the congregation.

My plan and initial practice was to say some introductory things about the RSV and proceed to use it in the weekly services. But from the beginning I sensed that there was a kind of tension and disease in the congregation when scripture was read. Nothing was said to the young preacher whom they had welcomed so warmly until the occasion of the first funeral. At its conclusion I was thanked by the widow of the elder we had just buried, who added an expression of regret that the scripture readings did not sound like "the Bible".

I began to grasp belatedly some of the implications of her unqualified reference to "the Bible". For her, what the King James said and the Elizabethan vocabulary and grammar with which it spoke were in reality the Bible. For her and generations in the past that speech and voice were the Bible. Christian education in their Sunday schools had been memorizing that voice. It was the language of Christmas and Easter, of their funerals and weddings. In fact, for forebears reaching back over three centuries this text and voice had been the reality they knew as "the Bible".

James Luther Mays is a distinguished Old Testament Professor and former president of the Society of Biblical Literature.

CHAPTER TWO

WHAT WAS THE
PRODUCT LIKE?

*But how will people meditate on something they cannot under-
stand? How will they understand something that is kept hidden
in an unknown language? As it is written, "If I don't understand
the language someone is using, we will be like foreigners to each
other" (1 Corinthians 14.11). The Apostle does not make an ex-
ception for any language, whether Hebrew as the oldest, or Greek
as the most versatile, or Latin as the most precise. It is only common sense to admit that all of us are plainly deaf in the languages
we do not understand. We turn a deaf ear to them. The Scythian
considered the Athenian, whom he did not understand, as barba-
rous. So also the Roman considered the Syrian and the Jew.*

*Translation is what opens the window, to let the light in. It breaks
the shell, so that we may eat the kernel. It pulls the curtain aside,
so that we may look into the most holy place. It removes the cover
from the well, so that we may get to the water; just as Jacob rolled
the stone away from the mouth of the well so the flocks of Laban
could be watered (Genesis 29.10). In fact, without a translation
in the common language, most people are like the children at
Jacob's well (which was deep) without a bucket or something to
draw the water with; or like the person mentioned by Isaiah who
was given a sealed book and told, "Please read this," and had to
answer, "I can not, because it is sealed" (Isaiah 29.11).*

From the preface to the King James Version.

23

Access to the Scriptures

The King James Bible was first and foremost a translation. The first instruction to the translators stated that this new Bible was to follow the Bishops' Bible as much as much as possible. But that Bible's language was difficult for ordinary people to understand. There were many words and phrases that were borrowed from the Latin and others which were not natural in English, and there were strange turns of phrase which the Puritans in particular despised (one said he would prefer to read the 'alKoran'). The language was lofty and pompous. Many people found its language obscure and laughable. It was the translation authorized for reading in church, but it was never loved.

The Qur'an is the sacred book of Islam.

Many have considered the King James Bible a revision, not only because of the first instruction. A comparison with the content of Tyndale's translation, for example, shows how much the King James owes that translation. When it was published in 1611, it was not registered in the records of the Stationer's Hall, which would normally have been done for any new book. But the King James Bible was considered a revision of the Bishops' Bible, not a new book, and therefore did not warrant being registered. This is a great pity as it means we do not know the month or date when it was actually released, how many copies were printed in the different editions, or even the cost of a copy. Yet the men who prepared this Bible considered it a new translation, as they made clear in the preface when they called themselves "The Translators."

As stated so eloquently in the quotation from the preface at the beginning of this chapter, the whole reason to translate the Bible is to give speakers of the target language access to the Scriptures. If the language is difficult to understand, or even leads to misinterpretations, then it is not doing what it was intended to do. If readers cannot understand a version of the Bible, then it is not properly translated into their language. If all they have are Greek and Hebrew texts, then the Bible is not available to them.

THE CHURCH AND THE LANGUAGE OF THE PEOPLE

When people have access to a Bible in their own, everyday language they are sure to interpret it in their own ways and develop their own understanding of what the Bible says. For this reason, the established church for much of its history had opposed translations into the language of the common people, reserving knowledge of the Bible for the educated clergy. In England, the first example of this opposition came when an Oxford professor named John Wycliffe (1320 – 1384) began to render the Bible into English. Wycliffe was well-known throughout Europe for his opposition to many of the teachings of the church which he felt were contrary to the Bible. He and his followers, called the Lollards, began to translate the Bible from the Latin Vulgate Bible because Wycliffe felt that the Bible was the possession of all Christians and should be available to all people in a language they could understand. The manuscripts from Wycliffe and his followers began to circulate in the 1380s, and a complete Bible that his young colleague John Purvey had assembled and revised appeared in 1388.

Some sources say the origin of the term "Lollard" is 'loll' meaning 'to idle', but others suggest it was an abusive term that meant 'mumbler', perhaps referring to their ideas that were considered heretical.

The Lollards' preaching, teaching and translating were early precursors of the Reformation. Wycliffe was opposed by monarchs and by the church, even to the degree that forty-four years after he had died, the Pope ordered Wycliffe's bones to be dug up, crushed, and scattered in a river. Free thinking was a threat to the established order, and the Pope believed that a Bible that anyone could read would lead to that.

Martin Luther (1483 – 1546), the German priest and theologian who is credited with starting the Reformation when he posted ninety-five theses on the door of the church in Wittenberg in 1517, believed strongly in the "priesthood of all believers." Because all Christians were priests, all should participate fully in corporate worship in a language they could understand. As a result, he undertook a translation of the Bible into German using a level of language that most German speakers would be able to understand. His New Testament appeared in 1522. The Bible which he and several collaborators prepared was published in 1534. The Pope and Church authorities opposed him and would have arrested him, but he was protected by benefactors, most notably the Elector of Saxony, Frederick III.

Luther was concerned with what he saw as clerical abuses, the worst being the way the church raised money by selling indulgences. An indulgence was a way people could buy forgiveness for sins. On October 31, 1517, Luther is said to have posted on the door of the church a list of ninety-five reasons why this was wrong, maintaining that forgiveness was a free gift from God, not something to be bought with money.

There was a view in the medieval church that people were divided into two classes, those who were temporal and those who were spiritual. The spiritual people, for example priests, had special standing in God's sight. Luther believed that all baptized Christians were priests and spiritual in the sight of God.

William Tyndale (about 1494 – 1536) met with opposition for the same reasons. Tyndale was the first English translator to base his work on Greek and Hebrew texts, and also the first to take advantage of the invention of the printing press. He, like Wycliffe and Luther, believed that the way to God was through God's word, and that the Bible should be available even to common people. Unable to get official permission to translate the Bible into English, Tyndale fled to Europe. He completed his New Testament in 1525 and it was published initially in 1526 in Worms, and later in Antwerp. Copies were smuggled into England and Scotland despite the opposition of the church leaders. Cardinal Wolsey condemned Tyndale as a heretic in 1529, forcing him into hiding. He was eventually arrested in Antwerp, held prisoner in Belgium at Vilvoorde outside of Brussels, tried as a heretic and then strangled at the stake and burned in 1536.

Thomas Wolsey (1471-1530) was a powerful English statesman and a cardinal of the Roman Catholic Church. He was a close advisor of King Henry VIII, but fell from favor when he would not cooperate with Henry's desire to get an annulment of his marriage to Catherine of Aragon. He built the Hampton Court Palace, the building where the Hampton Court Conference was held in 1603, at which time the decision was taken to prepare this new translation.

But the battle was essentially won. Within four years, four English translations, all based on Tyndale's work, were published in England. When James assumed the throne in 1603, he could see that a translation in English that was understandable and free of doctrinal notes could be instrumental in maintaining order in church and state.

UNDERSTANDING THE TEXT

By calling themselves "translators" in the preface to the Bible, the men who were preparing this new Bible were making it clear that more than trying to revise an earlier English translation; they were preparing a new translation from the original languages, albeit with reference to earlier translations.

Further, they were preparing a particular type of translation, specifically one that could be understood easily, and moreover, one that was meant to be understood aurally. They realized that people needed to understand the Bible when it was read aloud to them, as for example in the church service.

It is interesting to note that there is an implicit assumption that the translators did not expect many people to read this Bible for personal study. Most people would only hear the translation when it was read in churches.

Today the King James Bible is recognized as a masterpiece of elegant stately language which has consequently played a significant role in the development of English. But paradoxically it was precisely because the translators were trying to avoid literary excellence that they achieved exactly that. Certainly the level of language of the preface shows they were entirely capable of writing in the elevated style of their day. But they intended the translation itself to be understood by all people whether they were reading it themselves or hearing it read to them. They did not even mention literary elegance in the preface. By focusing on the greater goals of clarity and scholarly accuracy, the translators secondarily achieved literary distinction. For them, sense and meaning were the priority. But what is more elegant than simple clarity? If they made any assumption about the aesthetics of the language, it was simply that accuracy itself provided that quality. They aimed at truth; later generations recognized the beauty and elegance of what they produced.

KEEPING THE CONTEXT IN MIND

One possible key to the elegance of the King James Bible was that the translators refused to take a purely mechanical approach to translation, for example by automatically translating any particular Greek or Hebrew word in exactly the same way at every occurrence. They stated in the preface:

> [W]e have not tried to be consistent in translating words or phrases as some might wish. . . .But we thought it would be more fastidious than wise always to express the same idea with precisely the same word . . . Affecting such precision would breed scorn in the atheist rather than be useful to the godly reader.

They give several examples, asking why if they translated a Hebrew or Greek word once by *purpose* they couldn't elsewhere render it as *intent,* or if they used *journeying* in one place they couldn't use *traveling* someplace else. Implicit in their argument is that the words themselves are not sacred; God has used human language in all its diversity to communicate God's message to mankind. As the preface states:

> We cannot observe a better pattern of expression than God himself; who used different words without distinction in his holy scriptures when referring to the same thing. Unless we are superstitious, we may use the same liberty in our English versions of the Hebrew and Greek, based on the resources he has given us.

As they point out, there were "some" (perhaps scholars and clerics?) who would have preferred that they translate Hebrew and Greek words by the same English word at every occurrence. Even in translations being prepared today in English or in hundreds of other languages, there are some who want to do the same thing. But this ignores the fact that words can mean different things in different contexts. For example, the Greek word *sarx* which is frequently rendered as "flesh" is better translated "human nature," "body," or "humankind" in other places. The

Greek word *ekballō* was translated by the King James translators as "put out," "take out," "drive out," "cast out," "leave out," "tear out," "send out" and "break forth," just to name some of the ways they rendered it. Being consistent would not only make the translation sound very wooden, it would in fact fail to express the meaning clearly. Moreover, the King James translators felt such consistency would subject themselves to mockery from atheists. Non-believers, they felt, would scorn a text that did not use natural English. These critics could easily suggest that God's voice and message were limited. Further, the translators emphasize, being overly precise could actually obscure the rich nature of God's message. As they affirm, if God was free to use different words naturally, then so should the translators.

This decision allowed the translators to use a much wider range of the English vocabulary than otherwise would have been possible. Although this did lead to a lack of strict accuracy in some places, the great benefit was that it opened up the possibility of a much richer text than a more mechanical approach would have produced.

CHURCH LANGUAGE

The preface also criticizes the way the Puritans had rejected a number of ecclesiastical words such as *baptism* and *church*, using "washing" and "congregation." Clearly, of course, this was a political and theological decision as the King James translators were thereby conforming to traditional church language, something the Puritans were trying to move away from. But they also reject a number of borrowed words which the Roman Catholic Douai-Rheims translation had used. (They did not, however, mention that translation by name.) That version's *Azimes, Tunike, Holocausts* and *Pasche,* in the minds of the King James Translators were examples of language that kept that translation from being understood. "But," they state, "we want the Scripture to speak like itself, as it does in Hebrew, and be understood even by the uneducated."

> The purpose of this Roman Catholic translation was to uphold Catholic tradition in the face of the Protestant Reformation. To this end, the extensive notes were highly polemical. Although the King James translators would have had access to this translation, at least of the New Testament, it is pointedly not listed as one they referred to by name.

The king and his advisor Bancroft were not prepared to give any ground on this issue of traditional church language. William Tyndale had translated the Greek word *ecclesia* as "congregation," not "church," and *presbyteros* as "elder" rather than "priest." These differences were crucial to the meaning of the English Reformation. An "elder" would not have any ancient priestly significance, that is, would not necessarily be the means of passing on God's grace to humankind. Believing in the priesthood of all believers as most of the reformers did meant for them that there was no need for bishops and archbishops. Similarly, if *ecclesia* meant "congregation," not "church," then there was no need for the elaborate and expensive structure of the established church. As the preface shows, the translators accepted and defended the king's position in favor of traditional church language when it came to such matters of authority.

> One common understanding of "priest" is that this is a person who has the authority or power to perform religious rites, most notably sacrifices before a deity.

HEARING THE WORD

A common failing of many modern translations is the lack of attention to how a translation will sound when read aloud. But the King James translators focused on this, which surely accounts

31

for much of the continuing popularity of their translation, particularly in churches and contexts where oratorical elegance is valued, for example in the African American church.

King James had been clear about what kind of translation he wanted, and to a remarkable degree, that is what the translators produced. It was in the first place an accurate translation. James specified that it be accurate in relation to the originals, and the instructions and committee structures that he and Bancroft set up were designed to ensure that. By engaging more than fifty distinguished scholars and by putting in place multiple levels of checking, they assured that the translation was in the main stream of scholarship of that day, and was consistent in its approach to the original languages and to the translation principles agreed to.

The king also wanted the translation to be popular. He wanted the translators to use solid common English vocabulary, not Latin or Greek, and about 90 percent of the translation is Anglo-Saxon. It was to be readable in the idiom of that day. The translators were to retain the names of the prophets and other biblical characters as they were commonly used. If the translators had either translated some of the names, for example calling Theophilus "Friend of God," or had introduced transliterations that were closer to the original languages but not commonly used at that time, then the translation would not sound right and familiar to many ordinary people. It would be less "popular."

The translators were successful. Readers and hearers are still moved by the language of the King James Bible even when they fail to understand a passage or misunderstand it entirely. They still feel they hear God's voice in the elegance of the language.

Language Change

Because the translators were rendering the translation into the language of their time, they did not expect the translation

to have much longevity. Normally after just two or three generations a language evolves enough to warrant a new translation.
But as new generations continued to use the King James Bible,
they had to learn the older language, or, very commonly, they
simply misunderstood some texts. But the beauty of the language
guaranteed its continual usage despite this problem.

One study has shown more than 2,300 examples of words
or phrases that have different meanings in modern English
from their meaning in the King James Bible. "Prevent" as used
then meant "go before," coming from the Latin *prae,* "before," and *venire,* "to come." Psalm 119.147 was rendered "I
prevented the dawning of the morning," leaving present-day
readers clearly mystified. The Revised Standard Version trans-
lates the Hebrew as "I rise before dawn." The words "communicate" and "communication" occur a number of times where
contemporary English would have "share." Thus when Paul
in Galatians 2.2 "communicated" to the heads of the church
in Jerusalem the gospel which he was preaching among the
Gentiles, modern readers might miss what Paul was actually doing. Specifically, the Greek says that Paul "laid it before them"
with the view of coming to an agreement on this difficult question of principle and policy for the church. Paul explained or
"shared" with them the gospel message he was preaching to the
Gentiles.

NOTES AND COMMENT

James also insisted that this translation not be biased toward
any particular doctrinal position. Of course, the call for more
traditional ecclesiastical language is itself an example of taking a
theological position, although James did not see it that way. For
him, to use traditional ecclesiastical language meant the text was
unbiased. But the main thrust of this instruction was that there
were to be no interpretative notes. The only notes were to be
those that explained some Greek or Hebrew words which the
translators could not render easily without a rather cumbersome

expression which might even leave the meaning partly obscured. If there were multiple meanings of Greek or Hebrew words or if the manuscripts the translators had showed significant variations, then they could explain this in these notes.

James was reacting against the Geneva Bible of 1560, much loved and used by the Puritans. He did not object so much to the translation as to the many polemical and anti-monarchical notes that filled its margins. For example, both the Geneva Bible and the King James Bible render Psalm 105.15 as "Touch not mine anointed, and do my prophets no harm." The term "anointed" frequently refers to David or other kings of Israel, but the Geneva Bible adds a note that states that here the expression refers to the collective people of God, surely a subversive democratic notion in James's mind. By having no note here, the King James Bible allows the readers to assume that "mine anointed" refers to the king as it does elsewhere.

The Geneva Bible and the King James Bible are exactly alike in I Kings 9.12: "And he [that is, Rehoboam, who has just succeeded Solomon] said unto them, What counsel give ye that we may answer this people, who hath spoken to me, saying, Make the yoke which thy father did put upon us lighter?" As the text relates, Rehoboam disregarded the judgment and counsel of the older people, accepting instead the advice of the younger generation. A note in the Geneva Bible is an example of anti-monarchical bias: "There is no thing harder for them that are in authority than to bridle their affections and follow good counsel."

Proverbs 31.4 reads, "It is not for kings, O Lemuel, it is not for kings to drink wine, nor for princes, strong drink." The note in the Geneva Bible states, "That is, the king must not drink himself to wantonness and to neglect his office which is to execute justice." This note may have irritated James not only for its reprimand of a monarch, but perhaps also because he himself was at times known to over-indulge in alcohol.

A note that particularly incensed James was the one on Exodus 1.19. This passage tells how the Hebrew midwives explained to Pharaoh why they were not able to kill the Hebrew babies at birth as he had ordered. They said, "[b]ecause the Hebrew women are not as the women of Egypt, for they are lively, and are delivered ere the midwives come to them." The Geneva Bible defends this obvious lie in a note, "Their disobedience in this was lawful, but their deception is evil." James was obviously not going to agree with any note that suggested that disobeying a king was lawful. For him, disobeying a king was wicked, and lying about it only made it worse. He called the Geneva Bible notes, "very partial, untrue, seditious, and savouring too much of dangerous and traitorous conceits."

The instructions from Bancroft and the king stated that the only notes allowed would be ones explaining Greek and Hebrew words that could not be easily translated without a rather clumsy sentence, or some similar construction that still left some of the meaning obscure. But the translators went beyond that. As they state in the preface:

> It hath pleased God in his divine Providence here and there to scatter words and sentences of that difficulty and doubtfulness, not in doctrinal points that concern salvation (for in such it hath been vouched that the Scriptures are plain), but in matters of less moment, that fearfulness would better beseem us than confidence.

In other words, the translators felt it was important to alert their readers to places in the text where they were not really sure of the meaning. Frequently the uncertainty was due to textual problems, that is, there were places where reliable manuscripts disagreed. In the genealogy of Jesus in Matthew 1.1, the King James Bible has, "and Josias begat Jechonias," whereas the note reads, "some read Josias begat Jokim, and Jokim begat Jechonias."

The translators even argue that alternative translations can be helpful. "Alternative translations," they suggest, "are profitable for finding out the meaning of the Scriptures." Indeed, they go on to say that having an alternative reading in a marginal note beside a verse that is not clear "must not only be good but even necessary." "The wise would prefer a freedom of choice where there are differences of readings, rather than be restricted to one when there is an alternative."

Another type of example is Luke 17.36 which reads, "Two men shall be in the field; the one shall be taken and the other left." This verse was missing in most of the Greek texts that the translators had access to, but they realized that if they had not translated it, critics could accuse them of having left out a verse by mistake. So they had a note, "The 36th verse is wanting in most of the Greek copies."

In other places, the translators did not render an idiom literally. Instead they expressed it in simple, nonmetaphorical language and put the literal translation in a note. Isaiah 5.2 reads, "a very fruitful hill" but the note gives the literal rendering of the Hebrew, "the horne of the sonne of oyle." Readers of Isaiah 26.4, "Trust ye in the Lord forever, for in the Lord Jehovah is everlasting strength," will learn in a note that the Hebrew has "the rock of ages" for "everlasting strength."

What the translators did at Proverbs 26.10 is an especially interesting case. Here they rendered the text as, "The great God that formed all things, both rewardeth the fool, and rewardeth the transgressors." The note gives an alternate reading, "or a great man grieveth all, and he hireth a fool, he hireth also transgressors." What the marginal note makes clear is that the word "God" is not actually in the text. Here the Hebrew merely says "a great." Worse, the Hebrew is actually too unclear to translate with any degree of confidence. Some scholars believe the term means "archer" and others suggest it means "person in charge of something." Modern translations have rendered this verse very differently than either of the alternates offered in the King James Bible. Some contemporary readers criticize these modern versions because they differ significantly from the King James Bible, but if they had access to the original marginal notes and the preface (now omitted from most modern printings of the King James Bible), they would learn that the King James translators themselves had doubts about the meaning of this verse.

WHY THOSE ITALICS?

The translators used italic type to mark English words or sentence elements that good English required but were not part of Hebrew or Greek. For example, written Hebrew does not require the "it was" in the printed text in many sentences where natural English would require this. They rendered Genesis 1.4, "And God saw the light, that *it was* good." Written Hebrew does not require the "it was." Later generations of readers, particularly those whose Bibles did not have the preface or marginal notes, mistakenly understood these italics to be an indication of emphasis.

Compounding the problem is the fact that over the years, many publishers and editors italicized more and more words. This may have been because they misunderstood why the translators had used italics, it may have been from simple errors in composition, or possibly to emphasize certain words. Regardless, the result was that many later editions were very inconsistent. Many readers began to believe that the italics were for emphasis.

"[Readers do not] realise how much [the italics] have grown over the years. The original italics were thoroughly inadequate, and the modern proliferation remains an ineffective guide to the original text for the few readers who understand their intention." David Norton, *A Textual History of the King James Bible,* p. 162.

In the end, when the Bible was published in 1611 there were 8,422 marginal annotations. In the Old Testament, there were 4,111 notes that provided a more literal meaning of the Hebrew or Aramaic, and in the New Testament there were 112 places where the note gives a more literal rendering of the Greek than what the translators put in the body of the translation. There were also 138 similar notes in the Apocrypha.

THE APOCRYPHA

Many modern readers are surprised to discover that the King James Bible included the Apocrypha. This term refers to books that the church has considered useful but possibly not divinely inspired. All the early editions of the King James Bible included these books, as did Coverdale's translation, the Great Bible, the Geneva Bible and the Bishops' Bible. The Douai-Rheims also included it, as do Roman Catholic Bibles to this day. Starting in 1644, some editions of the King James Bible that were published in Amsterdam dropped the Apocrypha, and within a year or two some English publishers also stopped printing these. The first Bibles printed in Oxford, in 1675, did include these books, but in smaller print. Whether to include these books or not seems to have been the decision of individual printers. The British and Foreign Bible Society, founded in 1804, did include them until 1826, and the American Bible Society, founded in 1817, followed the lead of the British at that point. The main reason for not printing these books seems to have been a simple case of some Protestants rejecting anything which seemed Roman Catholic, though economics is surely a key factor as well.

MOVING FORWARD

The king also pushed the translators to work quickly, to get the work done speedily. He believed that having this new, popular translation was extremely important. No doubt some critics would have suggested that working quickly could result in a poorly done translation. But the several levels of review surely tended to overcome that. Many contemporary Bible translation projects have had similar results. Translations done in a relatively few years by committees with a good review process are more likely to be judged of good quality than translations which have taken many years with the input of fewer people.

Human Work Guided by God's Spirit

The preface, titled "The Translators to the Reader", was written by Dr. Myles Smith who later (1612) became Bishop of Gloucester. The thrust of the preface was not only to explain but also to defend the translation and many of the decisions they had taken. Smith describes the hopes he and the committee had for this translation and their convictions as to its value, and he defends it against attacks from some Roman Catholics for promoting translations that were obscure and purposefully difficult to understand. While he argues for the need for accuracy, he is critical of the Puritans for being overly scrupulous, wanting the same Greek or Hebrew word translated the same way every time.

The numerous quotations from the preface in this chapter make clear that anyone who really wants to understand the King James Bible would find the preface invaluable. Unfortunately, the majority of modern printings do not include it. Worse, there are features in the King James Bible which were explained in the preface, but which are now misunderstood because that explanation is missing. An example that we pointed out above is the fact that the translators were aware of differences in the texts of the original languages and in obscurities that remained, and they made it a point to inform their readers of these. Further, they were not endeavoring to create a work of literary merit, but were simply trying to express the meaning of the Greek and Hebrew texts that they had access to as accurately as they could in the language of the common people of that day.

Most significantly, the preface makes it clear that Smith and his colleagues understood that Bible translation is a very human process. They recognized their own human limitations and fallibility, and made a special effort in the preface to point that out. They recognized too that they were standing on the shoulders of translators and scholars who had gone before them – they did not see themselves as exceptionally gifted or guided by God's Spirit any more than their predecessors. But they did feel assured that God's Holy Spirit guided them in every aspect of their work. If readers in 2011 were aware of what the translators themselves said in 1611 about the art and practices of translation, and about their own translation, these contemporary readers would surely not be able to maintain some misconceptions. Rather than using the King James Bible as a basis to attack more recent translations, readers would recognize that the King James translators themselves would welcome the continued efforts to make the Scriptures accessible to each new generation.

CHAPTER THREE

PRINTINGS AND REVISIONS

Readers who compare King James Bibles available in America from different publishers may be surprised to find that they are not all the same. The Bible is being circulated in at least five different categories of editions, all with the same general content, but none completely identical with the others in a number of technical details. In addition, they differ in the pronunciation systems, spelling of proper names, verse style versus paragraph formatting, page and chapter headings, reference systems, printing the words of Jesus in red, and statements at the end of some Epistles.

One category is reprints of one of the 1611 editions. In 1987, Thomas Nelson Publishers in Nashville, Tennessee issued a reprint but in modern type. Hendrickson Publishers also issued a reprint in 2003. These editions can be studied for historical and comparative purposes, but because they would be so difficult for ordinary people to read, they were not intended for popular use. Both these editions include the Apocrypha in a separate section between the two Testaments, making them inclusive of all the content that was part of the original 1611 printing.

SPELLING, CAPITALIZATION AND PUNCTUATION

The King James Bible was published well before English spelling was standardized. A second category of editions encompasses several which show a surprising number of variants in spelling, capitalization, punctuation and use of italics. For example, the British publishers at Cambridge and Oxford and some American publishers including Thomas Nelson continue to use the capitalization of "Cherubims" that the 1611 had. In that version, it was capitalized in Genesis 3.24, but not elsewhere. They also retain the final "s" for plurals of words that are already plural in Hebrew. Examples are "Cherubims," "seraphims," "Nethinims," "Emims," and "Cherethims." The "im" in all these words is the plural marker in Hebrew. For example, the singular form of "cherubim" is "cherub." The added "s" really marks the words as plural twice, once in Hebrew and once in English. Other publishers have dropped this unnecessary "s."

English spelling had first developed in the seventh century, but after the Norman conquest in 1066, French became the official language and only a few monks continued to write English. The nobles and other wealthy people stopped speaking it, so that English was spoken primarily by people of the lower classes.

That changed in the middle of the fourteenth century when England began to establish its own identity after a long series of wars with France. The poet Geoffrey Chaucer attempted to develop a consistent spelling system, as did William Tyndale in his Bible translation of 1525. Both tried to develop a system that reflected how words were pronounced. But the literate aristocracy who were accustomed to writing in French undermined their efforts by continuing to use many French spellings, for example "double," "couple," "route," "sure," and "table."The aristocracy also attempted to pronounce certain words that were derived from French and Latin differently from the way the lower classes did. This, too, led them to spell some words as in French or Latin, not necessarily they way they were pronounced.

In 1619, Alexander Gil, headmaster of St. Paul's school, blamed the printers for the confusion. He wrote that "corruption in writing originated with the printing of our books, I lay all the blame for our chaotic spelling on the last." Publishers began publishing books in England in 1476, but nearly all these printers were European and they made many spelling errors. Since they were paid by the line, some of them added extra and unnecessary letters so they could earn more money.They also added extra letters at the end of lines to make them look better, for example "had" was sometimes spelled *hadde* and in other places *had*. Even the first English printer, William Caxton, was inconsistent in spelling. In a single passage of one of his books, he has both *booke* and *boke*, *axyd* and *axed*. Some of their spelling inconsistencies later became accepted.

Printers also contracted the spelling of the same words in different places to achieve an even column of text, for example using *ye* for *the,* replacing the Middle English letter called "thorn" which was the initial sound in a word such as "then," in contrast to the different sound in "thin."

In this period, printers set "v" for initial "u" and "v," and "u" for "u" and "v" everywhere else. For example "under" was written "vnder" and "have" was written "haue." The letter "j" occurs only after "i." Not until the 1630s did publishers begin to use "v" for consonants and "u" for vowels.

When William Tyndale's New Testament was published in 1525, the Pope and English bishops condemned it as sacrilegious. Tyndale had fled to Europe where European publishers who rarely spoke English introduced some inconsistencies. But Tyndale did also, and deliberately. In order to reduce the chance of censorship, Tyndale disguised his authorship by introducing different spellings so that authorities would think it was someone else's work.

By 1700 the English spelling system therefore had become more and more chaotic. A number of spelling guides appeared in the middle of the eighteenth century, but two dictionaries stand out as significant corrections to the problem. In England, Samuel Johnson released his dictionary in 1755. Johnson defined more than 40,000 words and in the words of his biographer James Boswell, "conferred stability" on the language - and at least with respect to spelling this seems to be so. In America, Noah Webster's *An American Dictionary of the English Language* which he published in 1828 tried to demonstrate that American English was different from British English and had its own standards. To a large degree, these efforts both achieved these goals and are landmarks in the standardization of spelling of the English language

The Cambridge and Oxford editions spell many words differently from the 1611 Bible, such as the more contemporary "chestnut" instead of "chesnut" in Genesis 30.37 and Ezekiel 31.8; "lunatic" for "lunatick" in Matthew 4.24; "crookbacked" for "crookbackt" in Leviticus 21.20; and "plaster" for "plaister" in Leviticus 14.42. Some versions, for example the American Bible Society, Oxford and Nelson, capitalize "spirit" in Genesis 1.2 and 2 Kings 2.16, whereas many others including Cambridge do not.

This is in part a theological issue. Using the capital "S" makes explicit that the translators understand the Hebrew word *ruach* to refer to God's Spirit, the Holy Spirit. The lower case "s" leaves open other interpretations. For example, the expression in

> Hebrew of "spirit of someone" often simply refers to that person, so "spirit of God" would mean the same as "God." Some contemporary translations render this word as "wind" or "power."

The 1611 Bible was very inconsistent in the use of the indefinite article "an" before the numeral "one," the nouns "harlot," "Hebrew," "husband" and "hill," and the adjectives "high" and "holy." However, it also used the article "a" three times, once each with "harlot," "high," and "hill." Oxford, Cambridge and Nelson follow the same pattern except they all have "an hill" at Isaiah 30.17, and "an harlot" at Joel 3.3. The phrase "such a one" occurs eleven times in the 1611 version, and "such an one" only twice. In the Cambridge, Oxford and Nelson texts, all instances but three have become "an." Holman had "an" in five cases. Zondervan and the American Bible Society used the article "a" everywhere. Holman retained "an" in fourteen cases and World did so in six cases.

PUBLISHERS AND MODIFICATIONS

A third category includes the editions of several American publishers who made their own modifications. For example, World of Grand Rapids, Michigan, a publisher eventually acquired by Thomas Nelson Publishers, printed the British form of the text in 1989 for the most part, but introduced several modifications. It has, for example, the modern American spelling for a number of words, including "hose" in Daniel 3.21, "chestnut" in Genesis 30.37 and Ezekiel 31.8, and "handiwork" in Psalm 19.1. Further, this edition capitalizes after a colon, as do those of the American Bible Society and Holman. World, Oxford, Cambridge and Zondervan on the other hand capitalize in some places where the American Bible Society does not, and different of the publishers capitalize after question marks, regardless of what the 1611 King James Bible did.

A fourth category is best represented by the American Bible Society which has moved in the direction of using currently accepted American spelling except for the old English pronouns and verbal forms, for example verbs with the suffix "-eth."

Zondervan also publishes an edition with digitized corrections of a text from the 1870s prepared by F.H.A. Scrivener in which he had eliminated notes added since 1611 but had attempted to make the spelling uniform. This edition also has the words of Jesus in red. Other revisions by the American Bible Society, Holman or World do not parallel the ones in this Zondervan edition. One of the features of this edition is to use paragraph marks (¶) but to continue writing each verse as a separate paragraph as the 1611 edition did. In fact, there is an extensive number of differences in this text and the other American and English publishers.

SUBMITTING THE MANUSCRIPT

Why all these differences? How did they originate? Is there one original King James Bible? The answer to these questions begins with an understanding of the printing technology of 1611.

After the various companies had finished their drafts, and these had been reviewed and revised by the other committees as the instructions had required, Myles Smith and Thomas Bilson gave the texts some final revisions and turned the manuscript over to Robert Barker, the king's printer, for publishing.

Smith (1554-1624) also wrote the preface that was described in the previous chapter. Known for his mastery of the biblical languages, he served on the first Oxford company which prepared the latter part of the Old Testament, and on the revision committee. Bilson (1547-1616) was the Bishop of Winchester. He had previously been a judge and a member of the Privy Council.

It is not clear exactly what Smith and Bilson gave to Barker. It may have been a manuscript, but it could also have been a marked up copy of the Bishops' Bible. There is very little evidence to support either idea, and most theories are sufficiently vague as to be inconclusive. What was said to be the "manuscript copy" of the Bible was sold twice during the 1600s, once to Cambridge University Press, and once to a firm of London printers. But this has now disappeared. Some speculate that it was burned in the Great Fire of London in 1666, but there is no conclusive evidence of this.

The Great Fire of London was a major disaster. Starting in a bakery, it burned through central London from September 2nd through 5th and destroyed the homes of 70,000 of the city's 80,000 inhabitants as well as many major buildings such as St. Paul's Cathedral.

Barker issued the Bible in 1611 in two separate editions, leaving bibliographers guessing which was the first. To add to the confusion, some sheets of one edition were bound with sheets of the other in some copies. The most striking difference is that in Ruth 3.15 one edition had "he went into the citie," and the other "she went." This has given rise to the names "The Great He Bible" and "The Great She Bible." Many contemporary scholars think that the "He" Bible was first and that "She" was a correction. Most current editions of the King James Bible therefore have "she," but the Revised and the American Revised Versions read "he." Also, the "She" Bible had "good pearls" at Matthew 13.45, but the "He" Bible had "goodly". The former had "the holy child" at Acts 4.27, in contrast with "thy holy," and "purified your selves" at 1 Peter 1.22 contrasted with "your souls." There were numerous other differences. One scholar has listed 658. Even the title pages differed in the two editions.

PRINTING IN 1611

The explanation for how these differences came about can be found in the printing methods of that day. Printers in 1611 had a limited supply of type. The custom was to set four pages, print as many copies as were needed for an edition, and then break down the type for further use. It was impossible to save what was set, as can be done today by computers. Nor could plates be stored as was done before computers. As a result, despite every precaution being taken, because of human fallibility, every edition would have some printing errors, and these would be different errors from those in other editions.

Proofreading was not done in any consistent manner, if at all. Printers put most of their effort and care into setting type and composing pages. One pattern was for the first sheet of a printing to be pulled off so that a "reading boy" could read the proof copy to the compositor even while printing was going on. Of course this allowed for many errors, as words could be misheard, spellings might be inconsistent, and homonyms, words that sounded alike, could confuse the matter even more. So there should be little surprise that the printed pages contained many errors. The matter was made worse by the fact that Bible printers were struggling with rising costs, and one way to reduce these was cut down on the number of proofreaders or lower their salaries. In fact, four of these working for Barker in the 1630s, fed up with having their pay cut, appealed to the then Archbishop of Canterbury, William Laud, asking him to intervene on their behalf.

Laud (1573 – 1645) was Archbishop of Canterbury from 1633 to 1645. He opposed many of the reforms that the Puritans wanted. As a strong supporter of the established Church of England and King Charles I, he was beheaded during the English civil wars.

NOTEWORTHY ERRORS

The first edition of the King James Bible that Oxford University Press published appeared in 1675. The Oxford printer John Baskett then prepared a very luxurious edition in 1682. But the high number of errors marred this Bible. For example, it referred to "The Parable of the Vinegar" instead of "The Parable of the Vineyard," which led critics to call it "The Vinegar Bible."

The translators had intended that any words inserted to improve the sense be printed in a different type face, normally italics. As one common situation, they added the copula, a form of the verb "to be," where written Hebrew did not need it although written English did. For example, the Hebrew of Genesis 2.23 is literally "This now bone of my bones." But to render this in English, the translators added "is" in italics: "This *is* now bone of my bones." Hebrew does not require the "it is" to be in print form because the reader of Hebrew understood and supplied it in reading. In another example, the Hebrew word for "dry land" is a single word, *yabbashah*. Following their rules, the King James translators had "dry *land*." Some later readers who did not know what the principle was assumed the translators put these words in italics to emphasize them. In the examples above, then, these readers might emphasize the "is" in the first case and "land" in the second. But as more and more editions were printed, that principle became confused and inconsistent, and often it is impossible to tell whether a word in italics was in the original Greek or Hebrew or not.

"The original italics were thoroughly inadequate, and the modern proliferation remains an ineffective guide to the original text for the few readers who understand their intention. . . . Bemusing, inadequate and ineffective, whether in the original or the current form, the italics only make reading more difficult." David Norton, *A Textual History of the King James Bible*, page 162.

Marginal references to other verses or passages in the Bible were also inaccurate in various editions. This was especially common in the Psalms where the references were made to the Vulgate numbering system, not to the numbering system in the King James Bible itself.

Misprints abounded. The most consequential was in an edition of 1631 where by accident the compositors dropped the word "not" from Exodus 20.14, so that it read "Thou shalt commit adultery." This edition became known as the "Wicked Bible." The blunder was spread in a number of copies. The king, Charles I, and the Archbishop of Canterbury at that time, George Abbot, were outraged that the Bible contained such a flagrant mistake. Robert Barker and Martin Lucas, the publishers, were summoned to the Star Chamber, an English court of law at the Palace of Westminster, where they were fined £300 and had their printer's license taken away. The majority of the Wicked Bibles copies were cancelled and burned, with only eleven copies surviving today.

Names were also given to many other Bibles with misprints. The "Judas Bible," a 1611 edition, has Judas, not Jesus, saying "Sit ye here while I go yonder and pray" in Matthew 26.36. It is possible that a disgruntled typesetter created the "Printers Bible," so called because Psalm 119.161 reads "Printers have persecuted me without cause." The first word should have been "Princes." The "Blasphemous Comma Bible" referred to several editions in which Luke 23.32 read "and there were also two other malefactors [crucified with Jesus]." This would make Jesus a malefactor. With the comma that should have been there, the verse reads "And there were also two other, malefactors."

Marginal Notes

One feature of the 1611 Bible was its use of marginal notes. The translators interpreted Bancroft's instructions about notes to allow notations and cross-references. The first edition had 6,637 marginal notes, of which 4,034 gave the literal meaning of the Hebrew and 77 of the Aramaic. 2,156 notes gave alternate readings of the original language texts. Sixty-three notes gave the meaning of proper names. There were thirty-one notes which explained the difference in the way a particular Hebrew text was written and the way it was pronounced. The New Testament had 767 notes. Of these, thirty-seven were variants in the Greek text, 582 were alternative translations, and 112 were more literal renderings of the Greek.

Following the first instruction Bancroft and the King gave them, the King James translators were using the Bishops' Bible as a starting point. This Bible and the others that the translators studied had relied to a very large extent on William Tyndale's translation, with the inevitable result that some problematic translations in that version were overlooked and perpetuated. For example, from Tyndale through to the Bishops' Bible Genesis 17.23 with some spelling variations read "as many as were men children amonge the men." The Douai of 1609 read "al the males of al the men." The King James Bible rendered the Hebrew text quite literally with "every male among the men of Abraham's house." Possibly the translators of the different Bibles did not ask themselves if a literal rendering of the Hebrew made sense here as they followed the pattern set by Tyndale. How many men were there in Abraham's house who were not males? "All the other males in his house" would be more natural English, something the translators were striving for throughout their work. The Jewish Publication Society *Tanakh,* a recent English translation, is also clear: "every male in Abraham's household."

Further, it was not uncommon for printers to introduce some "revisions" of their own as they spotted what they thought were errors in the manuscript or in the translation, or passages and words that might be misunderstood. For example, the original printing of Acts 24.26 in 1611 referred to Drusilla, the wife of the Roman governor Felix as "a Jew." In 1629 one printer altered this to "a Jewess," presumably to ensure that readers understood she was a female. The 1611 translation of Mark 10.18 read "there is no man good, but one, that is, God." Since there was the possibility that this implied that God was a human being, in 1638 this was changed to "there is none good but one, that is, God."

AN ORIGINAL KING JAMES VERSION?

As a result of all these issues, readers can rightfully ask, What was the original King James Version? Or even, Is there such a thing as an original King James Bible? The answer is quite simply, There is no such thing as a single, uniform, consistent, and flawless form of an original King James Bible. As we saw, even in 1611 there were two editions, a "She" Bible and a "He" Bible. The variations among the different editions continued to multiply. The lack of records available for inspection and the nature of publishing in the early seventeenth century make it impossible to fully determine for certain that the translators' preferences were ever fulfilled.

Further, although the King James Bible is referred to as the Authorized Version, especially in the United Kingdom, there is no evidence that it ever received any final written authorization from the bishops, the Privy Council, or the king. The Oxford English Dictionary traces the use of the title "our authorized version" to 1824, but one contemporary scholar has traced it to Ambrose Ussher who used it as early as 1620. Of course, the king had ordered that the translation be undertaken, but he does not seem to have given any final official approval to the translation, nor to its publication. The title page reads:

> *THE HOLY BIBLE, containing the Old Testament and the New. Newly translated out of the original tongues: and with the former translations diligently compared and revised by his Majesty's special commandment. Appointed to be read in Churches. Imprinted at London by Robert Barker, Printer to the King's most excellent majesty. Anno Domini 1611.*

Readers should note the word "translated"; it was not seen as a revision.

This translation was one "appointed to be read in churches." "Appointed" does not, however, imply that the work had been authorized for this purpose, as a modern English reader might assume. What this meant in seventeenth century English was that the work was laid out in a way suitable for public reading in churches. Many later editions dropped these words. The fact that it was to be read in churches proved significant, however, as this led to this translation influencing the population and the English language at large. Whether it was "authorized" or not, eventually this Bible was widely accepted and popular far longer than the translators anticipated. Its accuracy and clear language ensured that. Also, as more people became literate, it was increasingly used for personal study and devotional reading, not just for public reading.

FIRST PRINTINGS

The King James Bible appeared in 1611 in black letter type. This type face, also known as Gothic script, was archaic and therefore its very use was a political and religious statement. The more modern roman type was used for words that were supplied to clarify the text. It was printed in large folio size, fourteen by ten inches, three inches thick, and weighed about eighteen and a half pounds. Although published as a whole Bible, it was sold loose-leaf for 10 shillings or bound for 12 shillings. The New Testament was published in duodecimo size, which is about seven by five inches. It was also in black letter type.

A year later, the first quarto edition (about twelve by ten inches) and the first octavo edition (approximately nine by six inches) were published. These were both in roman type. Although they both reproduced misprints of the first edition including "hee" in Ruth 3.15, they did correct some other errors. (One printing of the 1612 in the octavo size did correct "hee" to "she.") Various other editions in the next three or four years show inconsistency in which some errors were corrected and some were retained, and in fact they also introduced new errors. The first duodecimo whole Bible was probably not published until 1617. A number of these smaller and later editions removed the words "Appointed to be read in Churches" from the title page, which may demonstrate that readers and publishers at that time did not consider the King James Bible as officially authorized.

It is not clear why exactly the publisher switched to roman type. It may be because it took up less space, possibly because it was easier to read, or possibly just to seem more modern and look more like the Geneva Bible.

Although Robert Barker was the printer of the 1611 edition, a number of other publishers quickly began to get permission to print the new translation. The university printers in Cambridge published the King James New Testament in 1628. The first edition of the entire Bible printed in Cambridge was published the following year by Thomas and John Buck. Some revisions and corrections to the text had been made, but there is no record of who carried them out. This was the first printing that read, "Take heed unto thyself and unto thy doctrine," in 1 Timothy 4.16, a change to the 1611 printing that had rendered *t didaskalia* "the doctrine." This is the reading that has continued in most editions of the King James Bible. Many modern translations have something such as "what you teach" similar to the rendering of the Buck edition in Cambridge which may be a better translation of the Greek, but is not how the translators rendered it. Another feature of this Bible was the inordinate use of italics, a practice which became recurrent through the years. For example, the Gospel of Matthew had forty-three italicized words in 1611, but by 1870 the number had grown to 583.

In 1633 the first printings of the King James Bible for Scotland appeared. There were a number of woodcuts inserted between the pages of some copies. This enraged the iconoclastic Puritans.

> Puritans placed considerable faith in language alone
> to define and order their world. They focused more
> on the verbal rituals than on visual images, which
> they violently rejected.

New printings brought new errors. One printing in 1637 by Thomas Buck and Roger Daniel, printers for the University of Cambridge, had "He called his sonne Jesus" instead of "He called his name Jesus" at Matthew 1.25; "shall up" instead of "shall rise up" at Matthew 12.42; and "thy doctrine" in 1 Timothy 4.16, not "the doctrine" as in the 1611 editions.

AN OFFICIAL REVISION

By royal command, a revision of the King James Bible was prepared by four men, Ward, Goad, Boyse (or Bois), and Mead and published in 1638 by Buck and Daniel. Ward and Boyse had been members of the translating committees who prepared the 1611 edition. The revisers made an effort to be uniform in the use of italics, but they also introduced several new readings. In Matthew 12.23, the original read "Is this the son of David?" They corrected this to "Is not this the son of David?" They also corrected Acts 6.3 to read, "whom ye may appoint" for "whom we may appoint" of the 1611 editions. But they continued the error at 1 Timothy 4.16. This Bible remained the standard text for Cambridge for 124 years until a revision by F.S. Paris appeared in 1762.

In 1640, the edition by Barker and the appointed representatives of John Bill is notable for using the letter *u* for the vowel and *v* for the consonant. This was also the last black letter folio edition.

The first edition printed abroad was in 1642 in Amsterdam. This edition had the notes of the Geneva Bible as well as annotations on Revelation by Francisco Junius, a Huguenot theologian.

Such an edition would have been impossible in England. After all, it was because he hated the Geneva notes that James had commissioned the new translation.

Franciscus Junius (1545-1602) was a Huguenot scholar and theologian. He had prepared notes on the Latin translation of Revelation which were incorporated into the Geneva Bible in 1599.

DATES IN THE BIBLE

Oxford did not begin to print the King James Bible until 1675. The dean of Christ Church from 1660 to 1686 and Bishop of Oxford from 1675 to 1686 was John Fell. In 1671 he had taken over management of the Oxford press and after much difficulty succeeded in receiving the privilege to print Bibles. A quarto size edition printed in 1675 contained Fell's spelling revisions. The Apocrypha was printed in smaller type than the rest of the Bible. A 1679 printing added dates in the margin, for example dating Job at 2400 BCE and the birth of Jesus at four thousand years after creation.

Other later printers also began to add dates to many passages and books. In 1701, William Lloyd, Bishop of Worcester, added the chronological dates and an index to the Oxford folio edition of the King James Bible, and for the next two hundred years, these dates were printed with only minor modification in English Bibles. The dates in Lloyd's Bible were dependent on the work of James Ussher, Archbishop of Armagh, and they continued to be inserted without authority in some printings for nearly four hundred years. These dates have been the cause of a great deal of confusion for many modern readers because of their discrepancy with modern scientific views. The American Bible Society stopped printing these dates about 1900, but World Publishing Company continued to print them in some editions right into mid twentieth century, as did the National Bible Press of Philadelphia.

SCRIVENER'S COLLATION

A number of printers continued the trend to modernize the King James Bible, updating spelling and punctuation, for example, and modifying the section headings. The Reverend F.H.A. Scrivener (1813 – 1891) was an important text critic and member of the committee which produced the Revised Version of the Bible in 1881. He evaluated the contributions of F.S. Paris, a Cambridge printer in the 1760s, and Benjamin Blayney at Clarendon Press a few years after that, each of whom had prepared a number of revisions in their editions, and asserted that they were the "great modernizer of the diction of the version." He also attempted to collate all the editions then in print and found more than 24,000 variations among them.

The Revised Version is discussed in Chapter Six.

In his own work of studying the Greek texts, Scrivener preferred the tradition on which the Textus Receptus had been based (called the Byzantine tradition) over more modern texts, although he drew clear distinctions between the Byzantine tradition and the Textus Receptus. His annotated Greek New Testament was published for many years, even into the twentieth century, in England as well as in the United States

The right to print Bibles remained in the Barker family until 1709. That right then passed on to Thomas Newcomb and Henry Hills, who held it for thirty years before it was acquired by John Baskett, and after that the right was given to yet other publishers. There was no printing and binding in Canada until 1943. The first in India was in 1944, done by the Calcutta Inland Printing Works of India on behalf of Eyre and Spottiswoode who held the right at that time. This edition was done for the British and Foreign Bible Society.

Printing in America

Prior to American independence, since the British crown held a monopoly on printing Bibles, all Bibles in America were imported. (The Geneva Bible brought over by the Puritans or Pilgrims was never printed in America.) The first English Bible printed in America was a King James Bible, printed by Robert Aitken in 1782. Aitken was a Scot who had settled in Philadelphia and was the official printer for the Journals of Congress of the U.S. Congress. At his request, Congress gave him permission to print this Bible, the only occasion of Congress authorizing the printing of a Bible.

"First English Bible" - an **Algonquin** Bible was printed in Cambridge, Mass. in 1663.

Following Aitken, after independence American printers did not honor the royal monopoly and a number of them began using available English Bibles as copy for their own publications. Of course, there was no central authority that could authorize a Bible for all of America. These printers not only retained the printing errors of English versions, but because of the typesetting methods then available, they even introduced a number of new errors. All printers therefore had their own versions with their own sets of errors.

The introduction of stereotype plates in 1804 greatly changed the printing process. The practice in 1611 was for printers to set type for four pages at a time, print them, then break up the type and set four more pages. Each time this was done, new errors could be introduced. Stereotyping involved making a mold of composed type in papier-mâché or other material so that a metal cast of the plate could be made. This led to a much speedier printing process, but also prevented the continual introduction of new errors in the typesetting process.

The Philadelphia Bible Society, founded in 1808, printed from stereotype plates they obtained from England, as did the Baltimore Bible Society that was founded in 1815. One American, David Bruce, went to England in 1812 to learn how to make the metal plates for stereotyping, and in 1815 helped produce the first Bible in America which had been printed from stereotype plates.

When the American Bible Society was founded in May 1816, one of its first actions was to have a Bible printed from these plates that same year. The society acquired its own presses in 1845 and began doing its own printing. There were already many variants in the Bibles printed in America reflecting some of the features of the British editions, but also some modernizations and corrections. In 1847 the American Bible Society Board of Managers set up a committee to prepare a more accurate text, especially dealing with page headings and chapter summaries. The committee compared their edition of 1833 with copies from Oxford, Cambridge, and Edinburgh, and reported on an astounding 24,000 variations in the copies they compared. This is similar to the number that Scrivener had found in the previous century. As the committee stated, "There is not one, which mars the integrity of the text, or affects any doctrine and precept of the Bible." In other words, they did not feel these variations changed the meaning of the text sufficiently to affect the doctrine or teaching. They issued a New Testament in 1850 and Bibles in 1852 and 1853 with the text they voted on as the Society's standards. One critic, A.C. Coxe of Baltimore, believed that it was not the business of the Society to revise the text, but only to circulate what was generally in use at the time. Although the committee making these corrections resigned in the wake of the controversy, the Bible Society formed a new committee which prepared a new standard text. In time the Society's text came to be considered standard by some publishers, whose editions often stated, "The Text Corrected According to the Standards of the American Bible Society" or something similar.

THE KING JAMES BIBLE TODAY

Many other innovations were introduced by the American Bible Society and other American publishers, including running page headings and section headings that were simple summaries of the text, American spelling, pronunciation marks on most proper names and the harmonizing of some Greek-based New Testament names with their more familiar Old Testament Hebraic forms. One significant innovation came at the end of the nineteenth century, possibly in 1895, when the National Bible Press of Philadelphia issued an edition in which the words of Jesus were in red type. This practice became extremely popular and soon Holman and other publishers including Thomas Nelson and Sons, followed suit.

As this brief description shows, there never was one original authentic King James Bible, and even today there are significant variations among published editions. The text continues to evolve, sometimes intentionally, sometimes accidentally. The twenty-first century cannot revert to seventeenth century usage, spelling, punctuation or even sentence structure. Rather than referring simply to the "Authorized King James Version," one needs to specify the particular stage of the text. Modifications have taken place in the past, and will continue. The question is, "To what degree can a literary work be changed and still carry the same name, still be seen as the same work?" Remarkably, however, regardless which edition a reader uses today, it will reflect to a very high degree the work of the six companies of translators.

CHAPTER FOUR

OVER THE YEARS

The King James Bible was a milestone in the development of the English language, and it shaped the religion and politics of much of the English speaking world for nearly four centuries. And yet this new Bible did not meet with immediate success and wide acclaim. When it was released in 1611, it made practically no impact on English society or on the church itself. Church and political leaders were concerned with other issues more than with this "revision" of the Bible. One of these was a controversy over predestination in the Netherlands and Belgium, a matter that was beginning to take a foothold in England, widening the division between church leaders who held opposing views on theological issues. What reaction there was to this new Bible was generally negative in tone, particularly from some scholars who were disgruntled that they had not been included in the translation companies, but also from the Puritans who continued to use the Geneva Bible.

Reduced to its key elements, predestination is a theological belief that God alone is Sovereign and all-knowing. Adherents believe that before creation, God determined the fate of the universe through all time and space and remains its sole Sovereign. For strict adherents, this included the conviction that God knew from the beginning of time which humans would accept his grace and which ones would turn away from it no matter how many times it was offered. The skeptics argued that the distinction between what God "foreknew" and what he "willed" seemed slight, and considered it inconceivable that a good and loving God would "will" any to perish. Adherents asserted that all humans had free will but that sinners, because of their adamancy, chose their unfortunate fate by rejecting God's grace. God's foreknowledge, for them, is not the same thing as God's desire that they remain "lost." The theology of predestination is particularly associated with John Calvin (1509 – 1564) and the Geneva branch of the Reformation. But roots of this doctrine go back to writings of St. Augustine of Hippo (354 – 430 CE), more than a thousand years earlier.

Some readers were so displeased that they called for an immediate revision of the King James Bible. These appeals were not taken seriously until the 1640s, and then for secular political reasons, not for linguistic, translational or theological problems. Most members of Parliament by that time were Puritans. They were unhappy that a Bible had been prepared under the authority of the king, for they believed only Parliament had the right to authorize a Bible for the people. They wanted to grant that authorization to the Geneva Bible, which had not been printed in England since 1616 when James put a halt to its publication. It was at this time that the King James Bible began to be called the Authorized Version. The Geneva Bible, however, continued to be imported from the Netherlands. After James died in 1625, his second son took the throne as Charles I. Charles was married to a French Roman Catholic princess, Henrietta Maria, and the Puritans were alarmed by the prospect of a monarch who was openly sympathetic to the Catholic Church. The Geneva Bible translation and notes supported the Puritan anti-monarchical position, while the King James Bible was seen as supporting the monarchy. This spurred many Puritan Members of Parliament to call for a new revision or translation.

The Parliamentary Grand Committee for Religion ordered a subcommittee to look into the matter. There were two categories of complaint: (1) the numerous misprints in all of the editions; (2) serious questions about the translation itself. One group in Parliament supported the claims of Henry Jessey (1601-1663), a scholar known for his competence in biblical languages, that the literary quality of the King James Bible was inferior.

Jessey spent most of his life dissenting against the established church, and was imprisoned several times, most notably when he was put in the Tower of London in 1640. He became convinced that immersion was the only biblical method of baptism, and then only for adult believers. He had himself baptized, and subsequently organized a church known as "Particular Baptists."

Other Puritans argued against the use of traditional church terminology such as "bishop," something that Richard Bancroft had specifically instructed the translators to do. Terms such as this were powerful reminders to the Puritan readers of the very church establishment that they were trying to overthrow. In addition, many of them wanted the Apocrypha to be removed.

A COMPROMISE

It is interesting that all this agitation did not serve to bring the Geneva Bible back into popularity. Its supporters recognized that in comparison to the King James Bible it was an inferior translation, but they wanted the Geneva Bible notes. The compromise was to print the King James Bible with the Geneva notes. Between 1642 and 1715 there were at least nine such editions released, eight of these in the Netherlands. But even this was unsatisfactory to the Puritans who continued to agitate for the replacement of the King James Bible. Geneva Bibles continued to be printed until 1644.

Between 1641 and 1651 there was a series of civil wars in England between supporters of Charles I and supporters of Parliament, most of whom were Puritans. Charles was eventually put on trial and executed in 1649, and in 1653 Parliament established a Protectorate under Oliver Cromwell. The monarchy was re-established in 1660 under Charles II, son of Charles I. The King James Version Bible was now respected as something that had its origins before the country was split by the wars, and was associated with the monarchy and antiquity. It now began to hold the same degree of authority for the English as the Latin had held for all of Western Europe for over a millennium. As such, it became an important symbol of England as God's country.

ACCEPTANCE IN AMERICA

Acceptance of the King James Bible in America followed a quite different path. Calvinist Christianity of that era put primacy on a sovereign and vengeful God and constantly doubted the validity of worldly governments. By emphasizing the differences between those who were chosen to be saved and the lost who would surely perish, adherents of this doctrine had little motivation for establishing strong and stable governments or founding a nation. The Geneva Bible notes and translation fueled these separatist inclinations, and the American Pilgrim Fathers carried these notions to North America. But as the country grew and spread, the northern and southern colonies lost some of their distinctiveness. Consequently, political processes developed and matured, and the need for a "separatist gospel" declined. In time, a need for a Bible that supported nation building supplanted one supporting separatism. So the "establishment" Bible, the King James Version, became the Bible of America, and by the end of the seventeenth century it was treasured as much by the British of the American colonies as by those at home, and was well on its way to becoming one of America's national texts.

The Language of the King James Version

Modern English speakers are aware of the fact that there are many dialects, accents and variations in the language, yet find these mutually intelligible for the most part, and recognize them as forms of English. It is even possible to talk about "standard English," a form which may be taught in schools throughout the English speaking world. But that has not always been the case. In the thirteenth and fourteenth centuries, for example, there were very great differences in the vocabulary and speech around the British Isles. Between roughly 1400 and 1800 the language evolved and changed in a number of remarkable ways. Most textbooks on the history of English agree that the two most important influences on these changes were the works of William Shakespeare (1564 – 1616) and the King James Bible of 1611.

Shakespeare was born in Stratford-upon-Avon in Warwickshire where he received his early education at a local grammar school. In 1591 he moved to London to become an actor, eventually becoming a partner in the company that built the Globe theater. He wrote plays which continue to be performed to this day, and poetry which is still widely read and enjoyed, particularly his many sonnets.

The English language scholar David Crystal writes: "All textbooks on the history of English agree that the two most important influences on the development of the language during the final decades of the Renaissance are the works of William Shakespeare (1564 – 1616) and the King James Bible of 1611. 'Influence' does not here refer to the way these works use language in a beautiful or memorable way. Extracts from both sources predominate in any collection of English quotations; but the present section is not primarily concerned with issues of aesthetic excellence or quotability. 'To be or not to be' is a quotatition, but it is unimportant in discussing the development of the language's grammar or vocabulary. On the other hand, Shakespeare's use of *obscene* (in *Richard II*) is not part of any especially memorable quotation, but it is the first recorded use of this word in English. . . . his usage would have been influential in developing popular awareness of it, and thus increasing its circulation."

"In the year that Shakespeare retired from writing for the stage, 1611, the 'Authorized Version' or King James Bible was published. It was never in fact authorized by any parliamentary process, but its title-page state that it was appointed to be read in churches through the kingdom, and in this way its influence on the population, and on the language at large, was to be far-reaching." David Crystal. *The Cambridge Encyclopedia of the English Language.* 1995. Pages 62, 64.

As the use of Latin faded throughout Western Europe in the late sixteenth century, the need arose for some sort of standardization of language to use in commerce, government and diplomacy. The French and Italians established academies with the express aim of standardizing their languages. In France, Cardinal Richelieu, the founder of the Académie Française, declared that among the Académie's goals was ensuring that French was "pure, eloquent, and capable of treating both arts and sciences."

Armand-Jean du Plessis (1585-1642) was Duc de Richelieu and a Cardinal in the Roman Catholic Church who served as Louis XIII's chief minister in France.

In England, however, the language was shaped not by an academy of elites but by a variety of influences. One was the growing availability of printed material. Dictionaries and books were increasingly readily available. It was not so much that the printers were striving for standardization, since there is evidence is that this did not really concern them. Rather, the more that published material was read, the more certain forms of the language came to be seen as standard. But most significantly, at this time when English was ready and open to some influence to help standardize the language, there appeared two great enduring bodies of work, both of which were meant to be heard. One was the literary work of William Shakespeare whose plays and poems are both aural arts. They were meant to be performed and heard. The other was the King James Bible whose translators envisioned aural readings of their translation within the context of public worship. Both addressed audiences that were appreciators of their own language, but largely illiterate.

NEW VOCABULARY

Shakespeare's impact on the language was primarily in vocabulary. Although he used English in beautiful and memorable ways – indeed all speakers of English regularly quote from his plays even without necessarily knowing they are doing so – when it comes to discussing the development of the English language it is his introduction of new words and new use of words that is noteworthy.

Shakespearean Lexical Firsts. Many words first recorded in Shakespeare that we continue to use include: accommodation, assassination, barefaced, countless, laughable, premeditated, submerged, courtship. There are also many words that did not survive such as abruption, exsufficate, vastidity.

Shakespeare also introduced many new idioms: what the dickens, as good luck would have it, salad days, to the manner born, cold comfort, love is blind – the list is extensive.

The King James Bible was influential in large part because it did not introduce many new words. In fact, by most counts it uses only about 8,000 different words, about half the number used by Shakespeare. It was purposefully conservative. The translators were aiming for a dignified, not popular style, and opted in many cases for older forms of the language even when more modern forms were available. But most important of all, they listened to final drafts of the translation being read aloud, verse by verse, in order to assess the rhythm and balance of the translation. It was meant to be heard. This was a preacher's Bible.

Of course, the King James translators did introduce many idioms into the language. But the translators were not so much creating them as Shakespeare was doing. Rather they were translating the biblical idioms from the Hebrew and Greek texts. It was the simple but elegant rendering of these idioms that made them so memorable and resulted in their continued use.

Here are some biblical idioms that are still known and used:

> my brother's keeper (Genesis 4);
> a good old age (Genesis 15);
> eye for eye (Exodus 21);
> to spy out the land (Numbers 13);
> the apple of his eye (Deuteronomy 32);
> a man after his own heart (1 Samuel 13);
> How are the mighty fallen (2 Samuel 1);
> a still small voice (1 Kings 19);
> the root of the matter (Job 19);
> by the skin of my teeth (Job 19);
> out of the mouth of babes (Psalm 8);
> go from strength to strength (Psalm 84);
> at their wit's end (Psalm 107);
> heap coals of fire upon his head (Proverbs 25);
> a lamb brought to the slaughter (Jeremiah 11);
> can the leopard change his spots? (Jeremiah 13);
> eat sour grapes (Ezekiel 24);

the salt of the earth (Matthew 5);
cast your pearls before swine (Matthew 7);
the straight and narrow (Matthew 7);
new wine in old bottles (Matthew 9);
the signs of the times (Matthew 16);
Physician, heal thyself (Luke 4);
all things to all men (1 Corinthians 9);
in the twinkling of an eye (1 Corinthians 15);
suffer fools gladly (2 Corinthians 11);
filthy lucre (1 Timothy 3);
(the love of) money is root of all evil
(1 Timothy 6);
the patience of Job (James 5);
rule with a rod of iron (Revelation 2).

LOOKING BACKWARDS

When it came to grammatical usage, the translators looked backwards, preserving many of the forms and constructions which were falling out of use elsewhere. For example, they retained many irregular verbs in their older forms: *digged* instead of "dug"; *gat* and *gotten* rather than "got"; *bare*, not "bore"; *spake* instead of the more contemporary "spoke"; *clave* not "cleft"; *holpen* for "helped"; *wist* instead of "knew." They also retained other forms that were already archaic, for example *brethren, kine,* and *twain.*

They also kept older word orders that had fallen – or were falling – out of use. Examples are *follow thou me, speak ye unto, cakes unleavened,* and *things eternal.* One particular example relates to the modern use of *do* with negatives and in questions. This is missing in the King James Bible, so we find *they knew him not* instead of "they did not know him," even though this latter form was already in use in the early 1600s. Shakespeare, for example, uses both the old and new constructions, and by 1700 the *do* construction was standard.

In this Bible, the third person singular of the present tense of verbs is always – *(e)th*. In most other texts from this period, this form had been replaced by – *s* – , a northern usage which was moving south in the sixteenth century. Both forms are found in Shakespeare.

Also during this period, the second person plural pronouns were changing. Originally *ye* was the subject form, and *you* was used as object or after a preposition. This is what we find in the King James Bible in sentences such as *Ye cannot serve God and Mammon. Therefore I say unto you . . .* But by 1600 in most writing *you* was already being used for *ye*, which soon disappeared from standard English except in some poetic and religious use. (The Bible, of course, had a role in influencing the religious use.)

Earlier, *thou* was the subject form, *thee* the object, and *thy* and *thine* were the possessives. Modern English would use "you," "your" and "yours." In early Middle English, *thou* was the singular form of *ye*. However, French was widely used in England during the Middle Ages, influencing English as a result. The English word "you" came to have the same associations as the French *vous* which is used for plural and for addressing a person who is not inferior or not an intimate friend or family member. Normally in French, the singular forms are used within the family or to address children and people of inferior social class. So English began to use *thou, thee* and *thy* in similar fashion. As in French, the plural forms *ye, you* and *your* were adopted as a mark of respect when addressing a social superior. By the sixteenth century, the use of the singular form to address a single individual had virtually disappeared, except in the case of family and inferiors. That is, addressing someone as "thou" could be a claim to being superior to that person or it could be a recognition of a degree of intimacy. God is addressed in prayer as "thou" as a mark of intimacy. This is the term someone would use when speaking to a family member. Examples would be Solomon's prayer of dedication in 1 Kings 8, Jesus' prayer in John 17, and in psalms such as Psalm 68.

It is interesting how in many churches and Christian traditions people address God in prayer with "thee," "thy," "thine" and "thou" in the conviction that they are being more respectful, the exact opposite of biblical use.

Middle English did not know the word *its* meaning "belonging to it." *His* was used meaning both "belonging to him" or "belonging to it." By 1600, however, *his* was used only for "belonging to him." But in the King James Bible, *his* is used for *its*, as in *if the salt has lost his savour, wherewith shall it be salted.* The same was true of the use of the genitive, so we see in the Bible *for Jesus Christ his sake.*

The genitive case is also known as the possessive case. It refers to the way one noun in a sentence is related to another, usually possessing it, as in "John's ball," but it can also relate to origin, as in "men of Rome," participation, as in "group of men," or a number of other relationships.

Another feature to note is how several prepositions are used differently today from what we find in the King James Bible. *Of* is particularly interesting, as in *the zeal of* ('for') *thine house, tempted of* ('by') *Satan, went forth of* ('from') *the Arke.* Other prepositions that were used differently from current English include *in* ('at') *a good old age, taken to (as a) wife,* and *like as* (meaning either 'like' or 'as') in the phrase *like as the sand of the sea.*

An is used before many nouns beginning with *h-* in a stressed syllable, such as *an hundred, an helpe, an harlot.* Wycliffe began this usage, and it was still used by some in the nineteenth century.

IMPACT OF A CONSERVATIVE STYLE

All these forms were already on the way out by the early 1600s, but the translators retained this conservative style. As they stated in the preface, they were not aiming to make a new translation, "but to make a good one better, or out of many good ones, one principal good one." By retaining older forms and traditional readings, especially taking usage from Tyndale and Coverdale, their translation could resonate with the past. This led them in many cases to opt for using older forms of the language, which explains also why in contrast to Shakespeare there are few new words in their work.

Using slightly older forms of the language gave the translation an air of familiarity. When people in 1611 read it, they were not faced with something that sounded modern and new. The King James Bible felt as if it had been around for some time. Most significantly, it sounded like English, not something foreign. Readers could easily lose sight of the fact it was a translation, and indeed, this was one reason many people rapidly begin to think of the King James Bible as "the Bible," that is, the authentic Word of God.

In his book *After* Babel, the philosopher George Steiner has described how the King James Bible came to be seen as something English, not a translation or something foreign: "In the history of the art very probably the most successful domestication is the King James Bible" (page 366). He speaks of the art of creating the sense of "at-homeness," a "native presence" for the text through translation strategies, most specifically by using language that was one or two generations earlier than their own. What they achieved could not have happened if they had tried to be "modern."

Consequently, readers simply began thinking of the King James Bible as having been written in English. In George Bernard Shaw's play *Pygmalion*, the character Henry Higgins tells Eliza Doolittle to remember, "You are a human being with a soul and the divine gift of articulate speech; that your native language is the language of Shakespeare and Milton and The Bible; and don't sit there crooning like a bilious pigeon." For Shaw and other English speakers, the King James Bible was "the Bible." The idea of inspiration, which was traditionally applied to the biblical texts in their original languages, now came to be applied to the King James Bible itself.

Shaw (1856 – 1950) was a dramatist, social activist and literary critic. He also advocated reforming the English spelling system, and left a part of his estate to that cause. He is the only person to have won both a Nobel Prize for Literature (1925) and an Oscar (1938) for his contribution to the script of the film *Pygmalion*.

In the 1960s, every summer thousands of college students earned money selling Bibles door-to-door. A frequent question people asked was "What do you think of these new Bibles? If the King James Bible was good enough for Saint Paul (or, Matthew, Mark, Luke and John), it's good enough for me." Or they might say, "I want the Bible in the language that God wrote it." (Personal testimony.)

The King James Bible was a milestone in the development of the English language. Albert Stanburrough Cook, a professor of English language and literature at Yale University at the early part of the twentieth century, wrote, "No other book has so penetrated and permeated the hearts and speech of the English race as has the Bible. What Homer was to the Greeks, and the Koran to the Arabs, that – or something not unlike it – the Bible has become to the English." The translation appeared at a time when Modern English was being established, and its use of clear English that all readers could understand led to it being foundational for the language. By striving for simplicity and clarity the translators unintentionally achieved enduring elegance.

Establishing Norms

Although it was not the intention of the translators or of King James, their Bible helped establish norms in written and spoken English. One reason was that the translators did not try to use language forms from all over England. Few forms from the English of the northern part of the country were used, as the translators kept to the language of the southeast of England where most of them were from. But it was standard literary language. The translators avoided variations of local dialects, which would easily have been confusing to many readers.

Probably more than any other language, English has the tendency to borrow from other languages and incorporate new vocabulary quickly. A fundamental contributing factor to this feature has been the influence of the King James Bible at this critical period in the language's development, the early seventeenth century. Many phrases translated literally from Hebrew, Greek or Latin were naturalized in English simply by dint of their frequent use in the Bible. "Biblical English" began to carry cultural authority. Part of the success was that the phrases borrowed from Latin were not intrusive in the otherwise Anglo-Saxon vocabulary. About ninety-three percent of the words used in the King James Bible are native English.

Literature

It has been said that great writers are first of all great readers. Their fluency arises from the reservoir of rich language that they have read which has then shaped their own use of language. What they have read has also given rise to the themes and motifs and understanding of their subjects. D.H. Lawrence (1885 – 1930), the English novelist and poet, has articulated this clearly:

> From earliest years right into manhood, like any other non-conformist child I had the Bible poured every day into my helpless consciousness, till there came a saturation point. Long before one could think or even vaguely

understand, this Bible language, these "portions" of the Bible were douched over the mind and consciousness, till they became soaked in; they became an influence which affected all the processes of emotion and thought.

"The Hills" is a Lawrence poem reflecting the language but disagreeing with the message of Psalm 121.1:

I lift up mine eyes unto the hills
and there they are, but no strength comes
from them to me.
Only from darkness
and ceasing to see
strength comes.

The King James Bible reads, "I will lift up mine eyes unto the hills, from whence cometh my help."

Lawrence quarreled intensively with the Bible, but the language of many of his poems and plays shows that it was very much influenced by the King James translation.

The poet Percy Bysshe Shelley (1799 – 1822) and his wife Mary Wollstonecraft Shelley (1797 – 1851), the novelist, short story writer and essayist, were both atheists, yet they read the King James Version aloud to each other in the evenings for entertainment. Lord Byron (1788 – 1824) had given up his Christian faith, but was influenced literarily by the King James Bible. Readers of his poems "Childe Harold's Pilgrimage" and "Hebrew Melodie" will hear the King James Bible in Byron's diction, and discover that the allusions are from the book of Isaiah.

Joseph Addison (1672 – 1719) was inspired by a Psalm from the King James Bible to write "Ode" in 1712, a poem which is still published in many hymnbooks.

Psalm 19.1 – 6.

The heavens declare the glory of God; and the firmament sheweth his handywork.

Day unto day uttereth speech, and night unto night sheweth knowledge.

There is no speech nor language, *where* their voice is not heard.

Their line is gone out through all the earth and their words to the end of the world. In them hath he set a tabernacle for the sun,

Which *is* as a bridegroom coming out of his chamber, *and* rejoiceth as a strong man to run a race.

His going forth *is* from the end of the heaven, and his circuit unto the ends of it: and there is nothing hid from the heat thereof.

Ode

The Spacious Firmament on high,
With all the blue Ethereal Sky,
And spangled Heav'ns, a Shining Frame,
Their great Original proclaim:
Th' unwearied Sun, from day to day,
Does his Creator's Pow'r display,
And publishes to every Land
The Work of an Almighty Hand.

Soon as the Evening Shades prevail,
The Moon takes up the wondrous Tale,
And nightly to the list'ning Earth

Repeats the Story of her Birth:
Whilst all the Stars that round her burn,
And all the Planets, in their turn,
Confirm the Tidings as they rowl,
And spread the Truth from Pole to Pole.
What though, in solemn Silence, all
Move round the dark terrestrial Ball?
What tho' nor real Voice nor Sound
Amid their radiant Orbs be found?

In Reason's Ear they all rejoice,
And utter forth a glorious Voice,
For ever singing, as they shine,
The Hand that made us is Divine.

Because of its aural nature, poetry readily shows the influence of the King James Bible. But it is reflected too in the works of many novelists. Charlotte Brontë (1816 – 1855) in her major novel *Jane Eyre* alludes to and quotes from the King James Bible repeatedly. Her general style was shaped by it. Brontë loved the Psalms, and the poetic parallelism that the King James Bible translators carried over from the original Hebrew of both the Psalms and Isaiah appears throughout her work.

By the early eighteenth century, at a time when public and private reading of the Bible was common and widespread, the King James Bible was the only translation that the culture knew. Consequently, its imagery and language were inevitably incorporated into the language and literature of English speakers everywhere. John Ruskin (1819 – 1900), an art critic and cultural historian, described how his own writing has been shaped by the prose of the King James Bible:

From Walter Scott's novels I might easily, as I grew older, have fallen to other people's novels; and Pope might, perhaps, have led me to take Johnson's English, or Gibbon's, as types of language; but, once knowing the 32nd of Deuteronomy, the 15th of First Corinthians, the Sermon on the Mount, and most of the Apocalypse, every syllable by heart, and having always a way of thinking with myself what words meant, it was not possible for me, even in the foolishest times of youth, to write entirely superficial or formal English.

CONTINUED INFLUENCE

In a recent book, the literary critic and Bible translator Robert Alter describes the continued influence of the King James Bible on the language and style of contemporary American writers:

> The King James Version was famously eloquent and a beautiful instrument for conveying the vision of the biblical writers to the English-speaking populace. Its distinctive style would in the case of many major writers, beginning as early as the seventeenth century, give literary English a new and memorable coloration. (The fact that it is often inaccurate, and that the eloquence is not entirely so unflagging as most readers remember, scarcely diminishes this broad impact.)
>
> Robert Alter, *Pen of Iron: American Prose and the King James Bible.* 2010. Page 1.

Despite the fact that there have been many English translations of the Bible since the King James Version in 1611, few of them have made any impact on novelists, poets and playwrights either in England, in the former British Commonwealth or in the United States. These writers continue overwhelmingly to mine the King James Version for its eloquent language and idiom which still sounds so good to the ear. This influence continued even when fewer and fewer people maintained a faith in the Scripture as divine revelation. Consequently, regardless of their religious or historical backgrounds, poets since the seventeenth century have echoed and emulated the resonant style of this version. This is due not only to the simple but elegant style of the translation itself, but also because it is this translation which has informed both the literature and common vocabulary of all English speakers in a way no other translation has. Thomas Macaulay (1800 – 1859), a British poet, historian and politician, said of the King James Version that it was "a book which, if everything else in our language should perish, would alone suffice to show the whole extent of its (the language's) beauty and power."

The Bible has always been a source of religious instruction, but in the case of the King James Bible, the language itself inspired readers to meditation and worship in a way that would have been impossible with dull or inelegant language. The twentieth century British novelist and philosopher Iris Murdoch (1919 – 1999) made this clear in writing of this translation and the Book of Common Prayer of 1662:

> . . . great pieces of literary good fortune, when language and spirit conjoined to produce a high unique religious eloquence. These books have been loved because of their inspired linguistic perfection. Treasured words encourage, console, and save.

THE TWENTIETH CENTURY

Many poems even in the latter part of the twentieth century reflect not only allusions and citations, but also the cadences and syntax of the King James Bible. Robert Frost (1874 – 1963), four time winner of the Pulitzer Prize for poetry (1924, 1931, 1937, 1943) can be considered an heir to the New England Puritans with his plain-style poetry that responded to Scripture with profound moral music.

Richard Wilbur is a contemporary American poet who has twice won the Pulitzer Prize for poetry (1957 and 1989). Many of his poems show that the language of the King James Bible influenced him. His poetry contains direct citations and borrowed phrasing, but the impact is seen also in the way he incorporates these into biblical parallelism and repetition. His poems often sound like the Psalms even if he is using New Testament themes. "A Christmas Hymn" is inspired by Luke 19:

> This child through David's city
> Shall ride in triumph by;
> The palm shall strew branches,
> And every stone shall cry.
> And every stone shall cry,
> Though heavy, dull, and dumb,
> And lie within the roadway
> To pave his kingdom come.

Another Richard Wilbur poem, "Ecclesiastes 11.1," also demonstrates a reliance on the King James Bible:

> We must cast our bread
> Upon the waters, as the
> Ancient preacher said,
>
> Trusting that it may
> Amply be restored to us
> After many a day.
>
> That old metaphor,
> Drawn from rice farming on the
> River's flooded shore,
>
> Helps us to believe
> That it's no great sin to give,
> Hoping to receive.
>
> Therefore I shall throw
> Broken bread, this sullen day,
> Out across the snow,

Betting crust and crumb
That birds will gather, and that
One more spring will come.

Both poems quoted with permission of Richard Wilbur.

In these and other poems, Wilbur uses direct citation and borrowed phrasing from the King James Bible, working them together with biblical parallelism and repetition to achieve a poem that evokes the Psalms in the King James Bible.

The King James Bible has not influenced only Christian poets such as Wilbur. Anthony Hecht (1923 – 2004), a Jewish writer who also won the Pulitzer Prize for poetry (in 1968) has drawn on the King James Bible for his allusions, themes and titles, and his sonorous language and phrasing are evocative of the language of the King James Bible. Howard Nemerov (1920 – 1991), another Pulitzer Prize winning Jewish poet (1978), did very much the same thing. At the end of his poem "Einstein and Freud and Jack" are these lines in which the language of the Kings James Version Ecclesiastes 12.12 and Psalm 51.17 are brought together:

Of making many books there is no end,
And like it saith in the book before that one,
What God wants, don't you forget it, Jack,
Is your contrite spirit, Jack, your broken heart.

In the King James Version, these verses read in part: "of making many books *there is* no end ;" and "a broken and contrite heart, O God, thou wilt not despise."

These examples show us that even while it may have been supplanted in many churches, the King James Bible continues to be a source of inspiration to many poets.

MUSIC

Every year during the Advent Season, millions of people around the world listen to large sections of the King James Bible being sung. Since its first performance in 1742, the Messiah of George Frideric Handel (1685 – 1759) has been a regular cultural event in churches and concert halls in countries around the world. The words of the libretto to this oratorio were taken directly from the King James Bible by Charles Jennens (1700 – 1773) except for selections from the Psalms which were taken from The Great Bible. One of the most memorable passages is from Isaiah 40:

> Comfort ye, comfort ye my people, saith your God.

> Speak ye comfortably to Jerusalem, and cry unto her, that her warfare is accomplished, that her iniquity is pardoned: for she hath received of the Lord's hand double for all her sins.

> The voice of him that crieth in the wilderness, prepare ye the way of the Lord, make straight in the desert a highway for our God.

> Every valley shall be exalted, and every mountain and hill shall be made low: and the crooked shall be made straight, and the rough places plain:

> And the glory of the Lord shall be revealed, and all flesh shall see *it* together: for the mouth of the Lord hath spoken *it*.

The voice said, Cry. And he said, What shall I cry? All flesh is grass, and all the goodliness thereof *is* as the flower of the field:

The grass withereth, the flower fadeth; because the spirit of the Lord bloweth upon it: surely the people *is* grass.

The grass withereth, the flower fadeth: but the word of our God shall stand for ever.

O Zion, that bringest good tidings, get thee up into the high mountain; O Jerusalem, that bringest good tidings, lift up they voice with strength; lift *it* up, be not afraid; say unto the cities of Judah, Behold your God!

Listeners who may never have read that passage have memorized the words "Comfort ye, my people." It is hard to imagine how any writer would not be stirred by the elegance of this exaltation.

The *Messiah* is the best known example of the King James Bible being set to music. But there are many other musical works that are regularly performed. And many are by recent composers. *Belshazzar's Feast* is a twentieth century oratorio by the English composer William Walton (1902 – 1983). Librettist Sir Francis Osbert Sacheverell Sitwell (1892 – 1969) drew on the book of Daniel and Psalm 137 in the King James Version for his text.

ORATORY

Both the work of William Shakespeare and the King James Bible had significant influence on poetry, literature and the development of the language itself, but in the case of oratory, it is this Bible that has proven to be more influential. Using about half the vocabulary of Shakespeare and intentionally using clear, common language that could be widely understood, especially when read aloud, the King James Bible has been a strong and powerful influence on public speakers. Its recurrent use in the churches gave it regular exposure. Especially in North American oratory, its language continues to resonate.

Lincoln's Second Inaugural Address is a masterpiece of oratory that drew extensively from the King James Bible.

"*FELLOW-COUNTRYMEN:* At this second appearing to take the oath of the Presidential office, there is less occasion for an extended address than there was at first. Then, a statement, somewhat in detail, of a course to be pursued, seemed fitting and proper. Now, at the expiration of four years, during which public declarations have been constantly called forth on every point and phase of the great contest which still absorbs the attention and engrosses the energies of the nation, little that is new could be presented. The progress of our arms, upon which all else chiefly depends, is as well known to the public as to myself; and it is, I trust, reasonably satisfactory and encouraging to all. With high hope for the future, no prediction in regard to it is ventured.

On the occasion corresponding to this four years ago, all thoughts were anxiously directed to an impending civil war. All dreaded it—all sought to avert it. While the inaugural address was being delivered from this place, devoted altogether to saving the Union without war, insurgent agents were in the city seeking to destroy it without war-seeking to dissolve the Union, and divide effects, by negotiation. Both parties deprecated war; but one of them would make war rather than let the nation survive; and the other would accept war rather than let it perish. And the war came.

One-eighth of the whole population were colored slaves, not distributed generally over the Union, but localized in the Southern part of it. These slaves constituted a peculiar and powerful interest. All knew that this interest was, somehow, the cause of the war. To strengthen, perpetuate, and extend this interest was the object for which the insurgents would rend the Union, even by war; while the Government claimed no right to do more than to restrict the territorial enlargement of it. Neither party expected for the war the magnitude or the duration which it has already attained. Neither anticipated that the cause of the conflict might cease with, or even before, the conflict itself should cease. Each looked for an easier triumph, and a result less fundamental and astounding. Both read the same Bible, and pray to the same God; and each invokes His aid against the other. It may seem strange that any men should dare to ask a just God's assistance in wringing their bread from the sweat of other men's faces; but let us judge not, that we be not judged. The prayers of both could not be answered—that of neither has been answered fully. The Almighty has His own purposes. "Woe unto the world because of offenses! for it must needs be that offenses come; but woe to that man by whom the offense cometh." If we shall suppose that American slavery is one of those offenses which, in the providence of God, must needs come, but which, having continued through His appointed time, He now wills to remove, and that He gives to both North and South this terrible war, as the woe due to those by whom the offense came, shall, we discern therein, any departure from those divine attributes which the believers in a living God always ascribe to Him? Fondly do we hope— fervently do we pray—that this mighty scourge of war may speedily pass away. Yet, if God wills that it continue until all the wealth piled by the bondman's two hundred and fifty years of unrequited toil shall be sunk, and until every drop of blood drawn with the lash shall be paid by another, drawn with the sword, as was said three thousand years ago, so still it must be said: "The judgments of the Lord are true and righteous altogether."

With malice toward none; with charity for all; with firmness in the right, as God gives us to see the right, let us strive on to finish the work we are in; to bind up the nation's wounds; to care for him who shall have borne the battle, and for his widow, and his orphan—to do all which may achieve and cherish a just and lasting peace among ourselves, and with all nations."

The address delivered by Abraham Lincoln in 1865 at his second inauguration is an example, as it drew extensively from the King James Bible. The words "wringing their bread from the sweat of other men's faces" are an allusion to the Fall of Man in the book of Genesis. As a result of Adam's sin, God tells Adam that henceforth "In the sweat of thy face shalt thou eat bread, till thou return unto the ground; for out of it wast thou taken: for dust thou art, and unto dust shalt thou return" (Gen. 3.19).

Lincoln's phrase, "but let us judge not, that we be not judged," alludes to the words of Jesus in Matthew 7.1, which in the King James Version reads, "Judge not, that ye be not judged."

Lincoln quotes another of the sayings of Jesus: "Woe unto the world because of offenses; for it must needs be that offenses come, but woe to that man by whom the offense cometh." The language comes from Matthew 18.7; a similar discourse by Jesus appears in Luke 17.1.

The quotation "the judgments of the Lord are true and righteous altogether" is from Psalm 19.9 in the King James Bible.

One of Lincoln's best known speeches is known by a quote from the King James Bible. In 1858 when he accepted the Republican nomination as candidate for the U. S. Senate, in his introductory remarks he paraphrased Matthew 12.25 and said, "A house divided against itself cannot stand."

The King James Bible has "every city or house divided against itself shall not stand."

Lincoln was hesitant to associate himself with any organized church, but he read the King James Bible extensively, and quoted from it regularly. Furthermore, he expected his audience to recognize the source of the quotations and allusions.

Similarly, some of the major speeches of the twentieth century show the influence of the oratory of the King James Bible. This would include John F. Kennedy's inaugural address and many of the speeches of Martin Luther King, Jr. The words, cadences, resonances and themes constantly reflect those of the King James Bible.

DEMOCRACY

Wycliffe, Tyndale and Luther were all persecuted for making the Bible accessible to common, ordinary people. These translators and reformers were all convinced, rightly, that if people read the Scriptures for themselves, they would think through theological issues for themselves and consequently have a deeper, more personal faith, and would also be able to avoid some of the errors and abuses of the established church of their day. The church leaders of their day understood this and, fearing an erosion of their control over the laity, tried to prevent these vernacular translations from being prepared or distributed.

Before the establishment of printing in Western Europe, most people did not know what the Bible actually said. The

Bible was expensive, not readily available, and in Latin. Once it was translated and printed in the languages of Europe, reformation in the church was inevitable. People could obtain the Bible easily, read it with comprehension, and decide for themselves what it meant. Historians point out that in England, for example, free discussion of the authority of the church and state helped bring about constitutional changes, leading to a monarchy with very limited rights and powers. And in America the climate of free and open discussion reached even greater heights and was one factor that led to the American colonial revolt. The Bible in English, specifically the King James Version, allowed and even gave authority to people to think for themselves. Quite possibly democracy as we know it would not have come about in Western Europe and North America without this. G.K. Chesterton (1874 – 1936), the Roman Catholic writer, once said of the English that they "did not really drive away the American colonists, nor were they driven. The [Americans] were led on by a light that went before." That light was the King James Bible. From it [readers] understood the equality of humankind. Each person was equally important and sacred, each one made in the image of God.

The German goldsmith Johannes Gutenberg developed movable type printing around 1440. However, the Chinese had begun using similar technology 400 years earlier.

Worship Language

Throughout the Christian church, the language of prayer reflects the influence of the King James Bible. The continued use of "thee," "thou, and "thine" in many churches, the frequent quotations of the benedictions and blessings in the epistles, the extensive use of the language of the Psalms – all these show the impact the King James Bible has had. It is perhaps most pronounced in churches of the Anglican tradition where the liturgy, prayers and collects are to a large degree based on the Bible. But when people from almost any theological orientation address God, phrases and allusions rooted in the King James Bible language frequently appear, regardless of what translation that church uses elsewhere in liturgy.

The church continues to sing the King James Bible. The hymn books of most denominations, even those which use only more contemporary translations in their lectionary and liturgy, are full of hymns that are based on the King James Bible.

Theological language is often based on the Bible. "Grace," "baptism," "blessed," "righteousness," "discipleship" – all these come from the King James Bible. Contemporary translations may use "kindness," "washing," "happy (or, favored)," "being right with God," or "following Jesus' teaching." But the older King James language persists when the church talks about its understanding of God.

KING JAMES VERSION ONLY

Some churches continue to use the King James Version in their worship and study to the exclusion of all other translations. For these churches, a great part of catechetical training involves teaching the language and vocabulary of the translation, and in explaining to children and new members the meaning of many passages that might be more readily understood in more contemporary translations.

A by-product of using the King James Bible is the perpetuation of gender bias. For example, when Paul addresses fellow believers or speaks of them, he commonly uses "brothers" even though it is clear that both men and women are included. Many contemporary translations will have "fellow believers" or "brothers and sisters" to reflect Paul's intention more accurately. Reflecting the Hebrew or Greek texts, "man" is used frequently for any person. Consequently, in Psalm 1, "Blessed is the man that walketh not in the counsel of the ungodly," the King James Bible mistakenly gives the notion that only males are being instructed toward righteousness. "Happy are those who do not follow the advice of evil people" (Good News Translation) includes men and women, a more accurate representation of the psalmist's message.

ENDURING USE

It is likely that pastors and other counselors will continue to use the King James Bible when offering comfort and consolation to people who grew up using this translation. Surely the familiar phrases will have more meaning to them in times of hardship, serious illness, death or loss.

The King James Bible continued to be known as the "new translation" even late in the seventeenth century, and it was still met with some misgivings even at the beginning of the eighteenth century, nearly one hundred years after its publication. Yet at some point, perhaps as late as 1750, there was a decisive shift in attitude and it began to be recognized as a great work of religious literature as well as the definitive English Bible. This attitude endured until approximately the 1920s. For the first 150 years, this translation was beset with criticism and suspicion; for the next 150 years, it basked in almost uncritical adulation.

CHAPTER FIVE

WORLDWIDE SPREAD AND USAGE

It is no exaggeration to say that the King James Bible spread around the world as a direct result of two parallel and overlapping movements: British colonial expansion and the modern missionary movement.

BRITISH EMPIRE BUILDING

The fifteenth and sixteenth centuries are often called the Age of Discovery. Portugal and Spain pioneered European exploration of the world, and established vast overseas empires in the process. As they saw the great wealth this brought, France, the Netherlands and England began to establish colonies and trade networks of their own in Asia and in the Americas. After a series of wars in the seventeenth and eighteenth centuries with the Netherlands and France, Britain emerged as the dominant colonial power in North America and India. Britain's loss of its thirteen most populous colonies in North America in 1783 at the conclusion of the Revolutionary War was a severe economic blow to the crown. Despite this setback, the British turned their attention to Africa, Asia and the Pacific. Britain defeated Napoleonic France in 1815, and for the next century enjoyed unchallenged global dominance, expanding its imperial holdings across the globe.

> **In 1707 the Act of Union formally joined England and Scotland as the Kingdom of Great Britain, under one monarch and ruling parliament.**

Colonization involved establishing some sort of government administration and a judicial system that is favorable to developing trade. For Britain, this also meant establishing the Church of England. As the government sent out civilian and military colonizers, the Church sent out priests and lay people to build and serve churches and schools in the British colonies. Not only did the British believe that it was their spiritual obligation to Christianize those they viewed as pagans and nonbelievers, they also understood the church to be a key means of controlling the native populations. They believed that accepting the tenets of Christianity was a major step for making colonized people "civilized," that is, more like Europeans. They also believed that Christianized people were less likely to revolt. The Anglican Church became the official church in these colonies. As such, the church worked hand in glove with the colonial administrators to form and maintain an orderly establishment, much as they had in the British Isles.

> **Churches outside of Britain that are associated with the Church of England are said to be Anglican, or part of the Anglican Communion.**

MODERN MISSIONARY MOVEMENT

In the latter part of the eighteenth century, what is generally known as the modern missionary movement emerged as an outgrowth of – and reaction to – the Enlightenment. This secular European philosophical movement placed its trust in the power of human reason, generating revolutionary innovations in political, religious and educational doctrines. It stimulated a great concern for political equality and social justice, based on the assumption that reason and science would solve all problems.

Because it focused on a personal faith in a Divine Being, religion found itself under attack from Enlightenment thinkers. One response of many believers was to couple their firm inner faith with a new concern for the world. For example, a Baptist minister named William Carey (1761 – 1834) articulated this when he published a paper in 1792 entitled *An Enquiry into the Obligations of Christians to Use Means for the Conversion of the Heathens.* Action followed this call. Carey himself founded the Baptist Missionary Society that same year, and the London Missionary Society was founded two years later. Within just a few years, a number of other mission organizations followed.

Among Anglicans, two early mission organizations focused their efforts primarily on North America. The first was the Society for the Promotion of Christian Knowledge, established in 1698, followed by the Society for the Propagation of the Gospel in Foreign Parts in 1701. The former, still in existence, had as its primary goal the publication of Christian literature. The latter organization, however, was formed in response to a study commissioned by the Bishop of London on the state of the Church of England in the North American colonies. The study found that the church in the colonies had little spiritual vitality and lacked good organization.

The best known missionary arm of the Church of England would come on the scene almost a century later, after American independence. This organization, the Church Mission Society, played a more significant role than the two earlier organizations in spreading the King James Bible. Founded in 1799, the Church Mission Society was an evangelical response to the Enlightenment, as was the case with the Baptist Missionary Society and the London Missionary Society. The Society was founded in Aldersgate Street in the City of London on 12 April 1799. Most of the founders were members of the Clapham Sect, a group of activist evangelical Christians. They included the Members of Parliament Henry Thornton and William Wilberforce who became known for his success in ending the slave trade. The founders of the mission were committed to three great enterprises: abolition of the slave trade, social reform at home and world evangelization.

The overseas mission work of the society began in Sierra Leone, Africa, in 1804, but spread rapidly to India, Canada, New Zealand and the Levant and North Africa. Its main areas of work in Africa were in Sierra Leone, Nigeria, Kenya, Tanganyika (now Tanzania), Uganda, Congo, Rwanda and Sudan; in Asia, the organization's involvement was principally in India, Pakistan, Ceylon (now Sri Lanka), China and Japan; and in the Middle East, it has worked in Palestine, Jordan, Iran and Egypt. The first missionaries they sent out were not English, however, but German, members of the Evangelical Lutheran Church in Wurttemberg.

The missionaries found themselves ministering and evangelizing in a number of ways: they preached, built churches and schools, established significant medical work, developed literacy programs, taught agriculture, and translated the Bible into hundreds of languages. Many were highly educated, and they also contributed to science as botanists, geologists, historians, anthropologists and linguists. Most of all, however, through their efforts, the Christian church was established in remote corners of the earth where it thrives to this day.

THE KING JAMES BIBLE AND NEW SPEAKERS OF ENGLISH

A significant result of this movement was that the growth of the British Empire coincided with the arrival of hundreds of missionaries in the colonies throughout the world. In most British colonies in the nineteenth and early twentieth centuries, both the established Anglican Church and an Anglican missionary organization were at work, as well as numerous other missionary organizations. All of these groups to some degree pursued two goals: to lead people to the Christian faith, and to establish European-style education. And all missionaries and administrators carried with them a common text, the King James Bible.

A key sphere of influence for the church was in education. The British knew they needed a corps of educated English speakers to work in the administration among the colonized peoples, and so they established schools throughout their empire. These schools were either founded and run by the church, or, in the majority of cases, funded by the government and administered by the churches and missions. Consequently, in addition to their work in evangelism and medicine, the missionaries became educators. In some cases they established their own schools, but they also managed and staffed schools for the British colonial government. The language of instruction was always English, as a principal goal was to produce an educated, loyal cadre of competent English speakers. The study of the English language and literature was compulsory. And so was religious studies and chapel attendance for the Christian students. The King James Bible was a foundational text of much of that education. It was presented both as a masterpiece of English literature and as basic text for study in religion classes. In this way even non-Christians were exposed to the King James Bible during their time at these elite schools.

There were some regions where the British did not insist on schools, for example in areas of West Africa that were primarily Muslim. This led to serious and unintentional consequences in Nigeria. Schools were widespread in the southern part of the country, but not in the Muslim north because the British had let the Emirs, the leaders, decide whether they wanted schools or not. At the time of independence, it was these educated southerners who were capable of running the civil service throughout the country, much to the resentment of the northerners. The massacre of many of these southerners in their midst was a factor leading to the Nigerian civil war from 1967 – 1970.

The contribution made by the Church Mission Society in spreading education in Kerala in the south of India, the most literate state in India, offers a good example of the impact the missions had. Many colleges and schools in Kerala and Tamil Nadu still have Church Mission Society in their names, for example the Church Mission Society College in Kottayam, a school that was a pioneer in popularizing higher education in India. Many high-ranking judges, professors, and government leaders in India were educated at the school, including the former Indian President of India, K.R. Narayanan. Most of these graduates were not Christians, but they learned about Christianity in the college.

Frequently, unless a translation had been prepared in the local vernacular language, new believers undergoing catechetical training had to learn how to read the King James Bible. This Bible was read aloud in all Protestant churches as part of the worship. And if an individual possessed an English Bible, it was almost certainly the King James Bible. Sunday School classes were often conducted in English, and memorization of Bible verses was from the King James Bible.

A testimony from a former British colony:

As I read your email, I was immediately reminded of my grandmother's funeral in the Cayman Islands in 1998. My father eulogized his own mother. Immediately after the eulogy, pallbearers marched the body/coffin out of the sanctuary. My father recited grandmother's favorite psalm (121): "I will lift up my eyes until the hills from whence cometh my help. My help cometh from the Lord, which (sic) made heaven and earth...." My siblings and I followed suit, since we had learned a number of the psalms as children. Of course, all of these memories of biblical passages are from the King James Version.

My religious and professional life has changed drastically since childhood experiences ... but the language of the KJV is still the only language of

memorized scriptural verses that remain in the isolated corners of my brain.
(Personal testimony of a New Testament scholar in New York City.)

Many Different Englishes

As a result of this exposure, to a degree not even possible in Britain, the English spoken by these colonized peoples became steeped in the vocabulary, poetry, idioms and cadence of the King James Bible. These educated English speakers often were only a minority of the population, but with their access to political and economic power, they formed an elite middle class in the colonies. They were the ones who served as technical, clerical and administrative staff in the private commercial sector and in the civil service. As people of prestige and position, their language, colored so significantly by the King James Bible, influenced the language usage of others who spoke at least some English. English idioms and metaphors derived from the King James Bible fill the speech of Nigerians, Ghanaians, Indians, Barbadians, Jamaicans and South Africans. An American or British visitor to West Africa, for example, might be surprised to hear an old word such as "vex" commonly used. It occurs several times in the King James Bible, for example Isaiah 63.10. Contemporary translations use "made sad" (Good News Translation) or "grieved" (New International Version). Sermons and political speeches follow the cadence and rhythms not only of indigenous languages the preachers and speakers might be familiar with, but also of the King James Bible.

In addition to the countries colonized by the British, American and British missionaries also carried the Bible into many other countries, for example Liberia in West Africa and the Philippines in the Asia. The

> **English of these areas was equally influenced by the King James Bible.**

In Ghana and Nigeria, a common place to see quotations from the King James Bible is on the front and sides of "mammy lorries" or "mammy wagons," vehicles that provide most of the passenger transport. Some of these signs that are seen frequently include "Watch and Pray" from Matthew 26.41; "Wages of Sin is Death" from Romans 6.23; "The Lord is My Shepherd" from Psalm 23.1; "God Never Sleeps" from Psalm 121.

Samuel Johnson, who prepared the dictionary of English in 1755 that helped standardize English spelling, reviewed an American book in 1756 and noted what he called so much "corruption" in American English. He expected that before long Americans would be speaking a language that would be unintelligible to people in Britain. A century later, in 1877, the British linguist Henry Sweet (1845 – 1912), wrote that he expected that within another one hundred years England, America and Australia would be speaking mutually unintelligible languages. And yet this has not happened. One reason is certainly the fact that radio, television and film have continued to give English speakers everywhere some basic models of the language. But it is also arguable that at the time of Johnson and then Sweet, the fact that all English speakers were being influenced to some degree by the King James Bible gave some stability to language change in many parts of the world.

The King James Version and Vernacular Translations

The missionaries were very aware that to communicate the gospel effectively they needed to use the local languages. They knew that the churches would be stronger if people were able to worship in their own language. So translating the Bible became one of their major tasks. The principal model they had for translating was the King James Bible. Indeed, many missionary translators who were not trained in Greek or Hebrew used this text as their base, that is, they were essentially translating the King James Bible, not the original language texts. Even those who had studied Greek and Hebrew tended to use the King James Bible as a model. As one African translator said to a translation consultant, "We didn't want our translation to sound significantly different from the King James Version. Otherwise it might not have been accepted as well."

As a result, many of these vernacular language translations that missionaries and converts prepared in the nineteenth and twentieth centuries are full of literal translations of the King James Bible. Because of the differences between the grammar and structure of these languages and that of English, these translations were difficult for native speakers to understand. For example, in the King James Bible, Jesus says to "bring forth therefore fruits meet for repentance" (Matthew 3.8). The meaning is "do the things that demonstrate that you have repented." American missionaries working in the Dogon language in Mali in West Africa retained the King James Bible form in the translation. Dogon Christians had been taught what the verse meant and had some understanding of the idiom, but when some non-Christians read this passage, they thought it meant that you were to carry fruit, perhaps oranges or mangoes, to meet someone on the path who was known as "Repentance." They stated they didn't know what this meant. The figurative meaning of "fruit" as "results" had been lost, and it is clear that these American missionaries were apparently unaware that "meet" in 1611 meant "worthy of." Further, Dogon did not normally have nouns ("repentance") that expressed actions. In this language it is necessary to specify who is doing the repenting. Since the translators had created an artificial word "repentance," the readers had to assume it referred to a thing or person they might meet on the path.

This example illustrates the influence the King James Bible had even in places that were not colonized by the English. (Mali had been under France.)

Authority

Many of these missionary translations came to have the same authority as the King James Bible to the degree that even today many readers still prefer these old versions over newer translations prepared using popular language and state-of-the-art translation principles. This is equally true for the way they perceive more contemporary English translations as for the new translations in the vernacular languages. These readers feel that the older translations are really God's Word in a way the new ones are not. For example, in Kenya many readers would rather read the older 1952 Union Swahili translation prepared by missionaries than use the *Habari Njema*, a newer translation (1996) in clear, natural Swahili. Further, when buying an English translation, it is still the King James Bible that these same people ask for.

On one fairly recent occasion, a group of church leaders in the Efik-speaking area of southeastern Nigeria were meeting to consider whether they should revise the Bible in the Efik language. One of the senior pastors was asked to read aloud a passage from one of the Old Testament Prophets in the Efik Bible and then describe what it was about. "I don't know," he said. "I'll have to read the English first to tell you what it means." The Efik was a translation based on the King James Bible, but to understand this version in his own language, the pastor had to first read the King James Bible in English. That was what he had studied and understood, and it was that Bible which continued to shape his preaching and study.

A Caribbean Example

Jamaica presents another good example. Until the 1990s, the King James Version was used widely in the religious education classes in most schools. Many Jamaicans resisted more contemporary translations. They felt that when it was suggested that they use translations that were easier to understand there was an implication that they didn't know English well enough to use the

King James Version. Others felt that these newer translations did not have the dignified poetic language of the King James Bible or the elegance of the King James Bible which so many Jamaican preachers emulated. But primarily, too many people felt that only the King James Bible was really the word of God.

This resistance carried over into translating Scriptures into the local creole language. By the late twentieth century, most Jamaicans spoke a distinct form of Caribbean English everywhere except in schools or very formal contexts. Because of the differences between this Jamaican English or Creole and Standard English, most speakers could read Standard English only with some difficulty. They found it even more difficult to understand the King James Bible. But in the 1990s when the Bible Society in the West Indies attempted to prepare Scripture booklets in Jamaican English, the churches and schools initially resisted their efforts. Standard English and King James Bible English had high status; Jamaican English had low status, and people simply did not want to read Scripture or other texts in the Creole even though this is what they spoke almost everywhere.

Some linguists had referred to "Caribbean English" as a patois, a term for a provincial dialect, often used disparagingly. Others described the language as a creole, a vernacular variety which is the result of contact with English. However, after independence and the growth of more sophisticated linguistic awareness of the complexity in creole languages, the tendency has been to view the variety spoken in several Caribbean countries as a language in its own right. In the case of Jamaican English, this is an example of what linguists call "diglossia." Frequently a language community will reserve a highly valued segment of their linguistic repertoire for situations they consider formal and guarded, and use less highly valued forms of the language in situations that are informal or intimate. These contrasting forms can reflect stylistic differences within a single language, as in the case with Standard English and Jamaican English just discussed, or they can present contrasting forms from two different languages. The latter situation exists in Paraguay where the common language is Guaraní, spoken everywhere, but where Spanish, the language of those in power, has prestige. Consequently, it is Spanish that people prefer to read.

Almost universally, people want to learn to read in the highly valued language. Inevitably, reading the Bible falls into this category, and in Jamaica it was specifically the King James Bible that was held in high esteem. By 2008, however, a project was underway to translate the whole Bible into Jamaican Creole, and with the help of the university and with publicity from some of the radio and television media more and more people had begun to accept the new Scripture materials.

LITERACY

In all the colonies, missions, churches and governments developed programs to increase literacy in English and in the local vernacular languages. In the indigenous languages, this involved developing writing systems, producing written materials, and developing programs to teach people to read. These programs were not always successful even when the writing systems and programs were developed well. It depended on whether people wanted to learn to read or not. If learning to read in the vernacular was the road to power or wealth, the program would be successful. But otherwise people wanted to learn to read the language of those who held the power, which in the British colonies was English.

In Africa, the principal reason people gave for wanting to learn to read was so that they could read the Bible, and in the English colonies, that Bible was the King James Version. It was common for people to learn to read the King James Bible but not to extend this skill to reading other materials. Dr. Eugene Nida of the American Bible Society told of one time in West Africa when a man was asked if he could read. "Of course," he replied, "I'm a Christian aren't I?"

This situation is not unique to Africa. When the American Bible Society did market research on illiteracy in the USA, as reason for wanting to learn to read, being able to read the Bible came out on top. Getting a driver's license and finding a better job were also major reasons.

Learning to read does not cause people to develop a new mode of thought, but having a written text may permit them to do something they could not do before, such as look back, study and interpret. As new Christians in the colonies began to study the Bible, they reached conclusions that did not always match what the missionaries intended or expected. One example in Africa was polygamy. Readers of the Bible saw that many of the patriarchs had more than one wife. As in Europe, the established church forbade polygamy, a ban which had posed a real problem for Africans. As more of them began to read the Bible for themselves, they established new churches which did allow this practice.

WANING INFLUENCE

Despite the continued popularity and use of the King James Bible by many readers around the world, the fact is that in most parts of the English speaking world, contemporary translations are now more widely used than the King James Bible. In Australia, India, Nigeria and New Zealand, for example, the Good News Bible and the New International Version are far more widely distributed than the King James Bible. These translations have made a great impact on the growth and life of the Church as people have been able to read the Scriptures with greater understanding than was possible before. But the King James Bible left its stamp on the English spoken in Britain's former colonies and on the literature and oratory of the churches. No contemporary translation can really be said to be influencing the language and literature as did the King James Bible. There are so many translations that no one of them can enjoy the dominance the King James Bible once did. When various Englishes were developing, for example Indian English, Caribbean English or Kenyan English, only the King James Bible was in place to influence their vocabulary and style. Significantly, too, today the major forces acting on language change and development are the electronic media such as television and radio. It is unlikely that ever again will one Bible translation play such a key role in the spread or development of English.

CHAPTER SIX

REVISIONS AND MODERN
TRANSLATIONS

The restoration of the monarchy that placed Charles II on the throne in 1660 put an end to the rivalry between the King James and Geneva Bibles. Despite the fact there were still many misprints and other errors that needed to be corrected, by this point few people were asking for a revision or replacement of the King James Bible. Charles's interest was in restoring the Church of England to its proper place as a stabilizing factor in English society and politics. The publication of a new Book of Common Prayer in 1662 and the regular use of the King James Bible helped ensure religious conformity that he felt was important if England was going to leave behind the division with the Puritans, the chaos of civil wars, and the period of Commonwealth.

The Book of Common Prayer is a type of book used in the Church of England and the Anglican Churches around the world with the words of structured, liturgical services of worship. For example, it normally contains the forms of service for daily and Sunday worship, including the Holy Communion or Eucharist, baptism, confirmation, marriage and funerals. It also sets out the Scripture readings to be read throughout the year. The 1662 edition used the King James Version of the Bible.

The King James Bible triumphed in part because of the elegance of its language and the excellent quality of the translation. But probably as important to its success was its association with the monarchy at a time when supporting the monarchy was once again seen as positive. Argument focused instead on the new version of the Book of Common Prayer, as more than 1,760 priests could not accept some of the language of the rites. This was the start of the continuing division between the Church of England and Nonconformists. But the King James Bible was used by Nonconformists and Anglicans alike.

After the Act of Uniformity in 1662, a Nonconformist was an English subject belonging to a non-Christian religion or any non-Anglican church. At the time, Presbyterians, Congregationalists, Baptists and Quakers fit this category. Later, Methodists, Unitarians and the Salvation Army were also considered Nonconformists. By 1851 there were as many Nonconformists as members of the Church of England.

However, in time all translations need to be revised or replaced since all are prepared with particular audiences in mind. Different generations and different audiences will need different translations. Readers who insist on retaining the King James Bible as the only or best English translation are actually ignoring the intentions of the King James translators who understood that the purpose of good translation is to render the Bible into the language as it is spoken by people at a specific time and context. As they said in the preface, it was their "desire that the Scripture may speak like itself, as in the language of Canaan, that it may be understood even of the very vulgar."

Here is an example of a word that has a different connotation today. "Vulgar" then referred to

ordinary people. It did not have the negative
connotation of today, "indecent" or "obscene."

By the time the King James Bible was a hundred years old
critics within the church and universities expressed an interest in
revising it. This trend continued for the next one hundred and
fifty years or more on both sides of the Atlantic. There were four
key reasons: language change, some unacceptable vocabulary, a
few theological issues, and the discovery of better Greek texts.

LANGUAGE CHANGE

The English language was changing and more and more readers were having difficulty understanding the King James Bible.
Alexander Campbell (1788 – 1866) was an evangelistic leader
during a period of revival in the United States in the period prior
to the Civil War. He compiled and published a translation of the
New Testament in 1826 and in the preface expressed why he felt
a new translation was needed: "A living language is continually
changing. We might as reasonably contend that men should appear in the public assemblies for worship with long beards, in
Jewish or Roman garments, as that the scriptures should be hand-
ed to us in a style perfectly antiquated, and consequently less
intelligible." Besides using contemporary vocabulary, Campbell
made a number of word changes that had theological significance. He used "institution" instead of "covenant," "overseer" instead of "bishop," and "servant" or "servant of the church" rather
than "deacon." By the time of his third revision in 1832, he had
moved toward a translation that could be identified as modern
English.

Alexander Campbell was born in Ireland, educated
in Scotland, but immigrated to the United States
when he was 21. Several American church groups

trace their origins to the revival he helped lead, including the Churches of Christ and the Disciples of Christ. He also founded Bethany College in Bethany, Virginia (now West Virginia), a school for ministers.

Although grammar and usage change over time, it is in the vocabulary that changes are most notable. In the King James Bible, the word "advertise" simply means "to tell;" "allege" means "prove," and "conversation" means "behavior." "Take thought" in 1611 meant "be anxious," and "meat" was a general term for "food." "Anon" and the expression "by and by" are translations of the Greek word which means "immediately." A contemporary reader faced with several hundred vocabulary items like this can easily misunderstand the text, or worse, simply lay the book aside as too difficult.

IMPOLITE LANGUAGE

By the nineteenth century many people wanted a revision because of some language in the Bible that bothered polite society. The problem really arose because of the very nature of the Bible. One reason the Bible can claim authority over believers' lives is that readers can identify with its personalities and characters. These vividly portrayed people are shown as fully human, capable of good and bad. The major characters in the Bible, for example Moses, Saul, David and Jeremiah, the ones who led the people at important times in history of the Hebrew people, were also deeply flawed. The Bible does not cover up ugliness; it presents virtue and sin alike.

Moses grew angry at the people when they were thirsty, but rather than putting trust in the Lord, he acted on his own and was told he would not be allowed to enter the promised land. David committed adultery and murder. Saul was insanely jealous and at one point consulted with a witch. Jeremiah complained bitterly to God for the way God treated him.

The Bible is also frank in describing the bodily functions and body parts. Sex, elimination, birth, death, sickness, genitalia – all are natural parts of being human, and mentions of each occur in the Bible. With few exceptions, the King James translators rendered these terms and actions in clear English. But by the 1800s some readers found the way these terms were rendered to be too explicit for good taste. As English and American society became more polite and cultivated, it was less acceptable to speak directly about these bodily parts and functions. Noah Webster (1758 – 1843), a great educator and the man responsible for the dictionary which helped establish American spelling, wrote that he found some language "so offensive, especially to females, as to create a reluctance in young persons to attend Bible classes and schools, in which they are required to read passages which cannot be repeated without a blush."

One case where the translators modified the language of the text is the Book of Ezekiel, where much of the language is deliberately offensive and shocking in the Hebrew, but much less so in the King James and most contemporary translations. Even so, many parents and teachers would not allow their young people to read this book. In fact, many rabbis also would not allow young people to read these passages.

Webster was also bothered by "incorrect" grammar. Consequently, he prepared an expurgated Bible that was published in 1833. This was an edition which had replaced offensive words and changed some of the grammar. He considered his revision of the King James Bible "the most important enterprise of my life." In his revision, he changed "they bruised the teats of their virginity" in Ezekiel 23.3 to "they were first corrupted." In 1 Kings 16.11 he changed "not one that pisseth against a wall" to "not one male." And in Luke 11.27 for "the paps which thou hast sucked" he has "the paps which nourished thee."

Here is part of Webster's introduction to his expurgated Bible:

The English version of the sacred scriptures now in general use was first published in the year 1611, in the reign of James I. Although the translators made many alterations in the language of former versions, yet no small part of the language is the same as that of the versions made in the reign of Queen Elizabeth.

In the present version, the language is, in general, correct and perspicuous; the genuine popular English of Saxon origin; peculiarly adapted to the subjects; and in many passages, uniting sublimity with beautiful simplicity. In my view, the general style of the version ought not to be altered.

But in the lapse of two or three centuries, changes have taken place which, in particular passages, impair the beauty; in others, obscure the sense, of the original languages. Some words have fallen into disuse; and the signification of others, in current popular use, is not the same now as it was when they were introduced into the version. The effect of these changes is, that some words are not understood by common readers, who have no access to commentaries, and who will always compose a great proportion of readers; while other words, being now used in a sense different from that which they had when the translation was made, present a wrong signification or false ideas. Whenever words are understood in a sense different from that which they had when introduced, and different from that of the original languages, they do not present to the reader the *Word of God*. This circumstance is very important, even in things not the most essential; and in essential points mistakes may be very injurious.

In my own view of this subject, a version of the scriptures for popular use should consist of words expressing the sense which is most common in popular usage, so that the *first ideas* suggested to the reader should be the true meaning of such words, according to the original languages. That many words in the present version fail to do this is certain. My principal aim is to remedy this evil.

The inaccuracies in grammar, such as *which* for *who*, *his* for *its*, *shall* for *will*, *should* for *would*, and others, are very numerous in the present version.

There are also some quaint and vulgar phrases which are not relished by those who love a pure style, and which are not in accordance with the general tenor of the language. To these may be added many words and phrases very offensive to delicacy and even to decency. In the opinion of all persons with whom I have conversed on this subject, such words and phrases ought not to be retained in the version. Language which cannot be uttered in company without a violation of decorum, or the rules of good breeding, exposes the scriptures to the scoffs of unbelievers, impairs their authority, and multiplies or confirms the enemies of our holy religion.

These considerations, with the approbation of respectable men, the friends of religion and good judges of this subject, have induced me to undertake the task of revising the language of the common version of the scriptures, and of presenting to the public an edition with such amendments, as will better express the true sense of the original

> languages, and remove objections to particular parts of the phraseology.

In all, Webster changed about 150 words and phrases. Many critics have wondered why he did not prepare a more extensive revision than he did, especially since he was a foremost expert in language use. One critic observed that Webster's revision "was one chiefly of the unimportant." The book did not sell well. But Webster faced the same situation that many other would-be revisers did, namely, that for most people the King James Bible was a classic work of English literature, much as Shakespeare's work was, and therefore should not be revised. Consequently, he only corrected what he as an educator saw as flaws.

BERNARD'S REVISION

A major revision of the King James Bible was published in Philadelphia in 1842. The title was, "The HOLY BIBLE; being the English Version of the Old and New Testaments, made by order of King James I., Carefully Revised and Amended, The Meaning of the Sacred Originals Being Given, in Accordance with the Best Translations and Most Approved Hebrew and Greek Lexicographers: by SEVERAL BIBLICAL SCHOLARS. Philadelphia: Published for David Bernard, by J.B. Lippincott. 1842." In the preface, the publisher gives several reasons for revising the King James Bible, many of which echo Noah Webster's concerns:

1. Lack of uniformity in spelling the same word;
2. Lack of consistency in translating words and phrases;
3. Archaic and obsolete terms and phrases;
4. Indelicate terms;

Errors. The publisher refers to Romans 6.17 in the King James Bible. "God be thanked that ye were the servants of sin, but ye have obeyed from the heart that form of doctrine which was delivered to you." He states, "Here God is thanked that the Roman converts had been the servants of sin, instead of being thanked for their conversion."

Important words that were left untranslated, by which he meant words that were transliterated from the Greek or Hebrew rather than translated. He refers specifically to the rendering of the Greek word *baptizō* as "baptize" in the King James Bible. This Philadelphia translation used "immerse" and "immersion."

To transliterate means simply to anglicize (in this case) the Greek or Hebrew word. Examples would be "angel" for *angelos* and "apostle" for *apostolos*. Translations of these words would be "messenger" and "sent person."

The preface to the New Testament was written by Asahel Clark Kendrick (1809 – 1895), the editor and translator. He maintained that he was not doctrinally motivated, and in other writings he defended the use of "immerse" and "immersion" as the best way to translate the word.

A THEOLOGICAL DISPUTE

Throughout the nineteenth century, scholars, publishers, and ministers produced revisions of the King James Bible. A revision of the New Testament published in 1850 prepared by Spencer H. Cone (1785 – 1855) and W.H. Wyckoff (1807 – 1877) attempted to improve both the translation and the original texts followed by the King James translators. That is, they felt there were some errors in the translation itself that needed correcting, and they wanted to base the translation on better Greek texts than had been available to the King James translators. Cone, a Baptist minister, was Corresponding Secretary of the American Bible Society from 1833 to 1836. He became involved in a controversy over the use of "immerse" instead of "baptize." The American Bible Society refused to finance the printing of a Bible in Bengali that used the Bengali word for "immerse" instead of transliterating "baptism." Cone resigned from the Society and helped found the American and Foreign Bible Society in 1836. Some members of the new organization pushed for a translation in English that used "immerse" and "immersion." Interestingly, the Baptist missionary Adoniram Judson (1788 – 1850) who had prepared the Bengali translation with "immerse," was himself opposed to changing "baptism" in the King James Bible. In the end, the newly formed organization rejected the proposal, so in 1850 Cone helped found the American Bible Union whose express purpose was to produce an "immersionist" revision of the King James New Bible. Cone joined up with Wyckoff, editor of *The Baptist Advocate,* to prepare this revision. In addition to using "immerse" they made several hundred other changes to the text, but they considered their revision only a temporary measure until a fuller revision could be done.

Judson, originally a Congregationalist and later a Baptist, was the first Protestant American missionary to remain long enough in Burma to establish a mission there.

There were a number of other "immersionist" translations produced that explicitly took a doctrinal position over this issue, including a New Testament by the Adventist Nathan Whiting in 1849; a New Testament by H.T. Anderson of the Disciples of Christ in 1864; the Baptist Samuel Williams in 1881; Cortes Jackson, also of the Disciples of Christ, in 1883; and a Universalist minister, J.W. Hanson in 1884-1885.

The American and Foreign Bible Society that Cone helped found produced another revision of the King James Bible that used modern spelling. The New Testament appeared in 1838 and the whole Bible in 1839. One feature of this revision was a table of the meaning of certain difficult words. There were three columns, one with the Greek, a second giving the King James Version rendering, and a third displaying the "Proper Meaning." Some of the words listed are "angel" (messenger), "baptism/baptize" (immersion/immerse), "bishop" (overseer), "charity" (love), "church" (organization) and "Easter" (Passover).

BETTER GREEK TEXTS

The discovery in the nineteenth century of Greek manuscripts that were six hundred to a thousand years closer to the original writings gave further impetus to the call for revising the King James Bible, especially the New Testament. Textual scholars were beginning to understand that the texts that were available to the King James translators had many significant differences with these older, more reliable texts. Alexander Campbell was one of the first to recognize the relevance of this for revising the King James Bible. He wrote in the preface to his 1826 translation of the New Testament, "We are now in possession of much better means of making an exact translation than we were at the time when the common version [King James Version] appeared." His translation did not display great style, but he opened the door for other translators and revisers to base their translations on a better Greek text, and also to use more natural contemporary English.

Textual critics examine the many variations in manuscripts that are available and try to establish a "critical edition," one containing a text most closely approximating the original. Other scholars may choose to base their work on one particular manuscript or stage of development. The King James

> translators based their New Testament on the Textus
> Receptus, the best that was available to them at the
> time, but which was not very old. Essentially, the
> need for critical texts arose much later when more
> manuscripts were discovered.

All who contemplated revising the King James Bible found themselves in something of a dilemma. On the one hand, it was clear that for the translation to communicate effectively to the readers of a new generation, a revision incorporating new renderings was needed. Additionally, some of the translation and textual errors needed to be corrected. On the other hand, the King James Bible had achieved iconic status. If it was a great masterpiece of English literature, if it really was the definitive translation in English of the Holy Scriptures, how could it be replaced?

REVISED VERSION

Nevertheless, there were intrepid scholars who were willing to undertake revisions. In 1870, a motion was presented to the Upper House of Convocation of the Southern Province of Canterbury in the Church of England calling for a committee to be formed to revise the "Authorized Version," that is, the King James Version. The motion called for correcting "plain and clear errors, whether in the Hebrew or Greek text originally adopted by the translators, or in the translation made from the same, shall on due investigation, be found to exist." The motion was eventually adopted. It specified that a new translation was not contemplated, nor even any alteration of the language, "except where, in the judgement of the most competent scholars, such change is necessary."

By 1880, two committees were set up with twenty-eight revisers for the Old Testament and twenty-four for the New. The first principle these revisers adopted was "to introduce as few alterations as possible, consistently with faithfulness." They listed five different kinds of alterations: (1) ones based on Greek texts different from the ones that the King James Bible had followed; (2) places where the King James Bible was wrong; (3) places where the King James Bible was ambiguous; (4) places where the King James Bible was inconsistent in translating parallel passages; (5) alterations which were required by changes that had already been made, although these did not necessarily make the revision more faithful.

For the Greek text of the New Testament, the revisers followed the text being prepared by B.F. Westcott and F.J.A. Hort. The Westcott and Hort Greek New Testament was not actually published until five days before the revision, but the two scholars had generously made the results of their work available to the revisers.

Westcott (1825 – 1901) and Hort (1828 – 1892) worked together for 28 years, carefully studying and evaluating the many Greek texts that had become available. Their text was published in 1881, and revised in 1892. Their work was of such quality that even when the United Bible Societies organized a major project in 1954 to prepare a Greek New Testament that evaluated all extant Greek manuscripts and sources, the committee took the Westcott and Hort text as their starting point.

When the New Testament of what would be called the Revised Bible appeared in May of 1881, the revisers had made 5,788 changes in the New Testament on the basis of the Greek text, and 36,191 changes for other reasons. The New Testament was published in the United States just three days after it was released in England. The Chicago *Tribune* and Chicago *Times* newspapers published the whole text of the New Testament in special Sunday supplements on May 22 of that year. Within one year, three million copies of the New Testament were sold in Great Britain and America.

The Old Testament was published in 1885. At first, there were no plans to revise the Apocrypha. But since these books in the King James Bible had been translated in haste – and not very well – the New Testament translation team, working in groups, undertook the revision of the Apocrypha after completing their work on the New Testament. It was published in 1894. The revision of the Apocrypha doesn't seem to have fared much better than the King James Bible Apocrypha had. One scholar suggested that it showed signs of having been done by tired men.

AMERICAN STANDARD VERSION

The British recognized the increasing importance of the work of American scholars, and shortly after the Revised Bible project began, they invited Philip Schaff (1819 – 1893) of Union Theological Seminary in New York City to develop some guidelines for American participation in the revision project. This led to the formation of the American Revision Committee in 1871. Ultimately, the Americans would not be happy with the way their suggestions were handled by the British. The British work was sent to the Americans who then returned their comments. The same process was followed for a second and then a third revision, but American proposals had to have the approval of two-thirds of the British revisers in order to be accepted.

> Philip Schaff was Swiss-born German trained church historian. He had first moved to the United States to teach at a German Reformed seminary in Mercersburg, Pennsylvania.

One particular point of contention was the appendix. The British had agreed that an appendix would contain a number of important references that the Americans wanted but which were not ultimately adopted. When the Bible was published in 1881, the appendix was not the one the Americans had approved, and it had a very misleading heading, "List of Readings and Renderings Preferred by the American Committee Recorded at their Desire." In the minds of the Americans, this made it seem that the only points of difference between the two committees were those included in the appendix.

The Americans did not make a public protest since they did not want to hurt sales of the revision, but it strengthened their resolve to prepare an American revision. They had agreed they would not prepare one of their own for fourteen years after the release of the British Revised Version. Their committee continued their work, and after the fourteen years had passed, released the American Standard Version in 1901. This edition listed the points of difference with the British Revised Version in the appendix.

The Americans felt that the British Revised Version had retained too many obsolete words, such as "sith," "holpen," "bewray," "grisled," "hough" and "marish." They also were aware of some vocabulary items that were different in British and American English. For example, "corn" in British English was better rendered "grain" in America, "chargers" in America were "horses," "chapmen" were "traders," and "occupiers" were "merchants." The Americans also rendered a number of verses differently. For example in Acts 17.22 the British version had "too superstitious" but the Americans had "very religious." And in Acts 26.28, the American version has "With but little persuasion thou wouldest fain make me a Christian," which is perhaps more accurate than the British "Almost thou persuadest me to be a Christian."

Thomas Nelson and Sons became the exclusive owner of the copyright of the American Standard Version. This was later passed on to the International Council of Religious Education, which subsequently became the Department of Christian Education of the National Council of the Churches of Christ in the United States.

IMPACT OF THE REVISED VERSION AND THE AMERICAN STANDARD VERSION

The Revised Bible and the American Standard Version were each intended to be only a modest revision of the King James Bible. The revisers in both Britain and the United States tried to follow the same principles of translation as the King James translators. In particular, they understood the concept of faithfulness to mean they should follow the order of the Hebrew or Greek words rather than impose one that would be more natural to English. They even rendered the definite and indefinite articles and tenses in ways that simply did not conform to contemporary English usage. The result was that these revisions are examples of translation English, what is sometimes called "translationese." Worse, in some cases the revisers used out-of-date language that was never part of the King James Bible.

As used by scholars, "translationese" has become a technical word to describe a translation that is awkward and ungrammatical because the translators have been overly literal in the idioms and syntax.

On the positive side, for the most part the revisers eliminated the misleading practice of using italics for words in the translation which were not required in Hebrew or Greek grammar. They also abandoned the practice of setting each verse as a new paragraph. In most cases, the poetic passages in prose books were actually printed as poetry, a helpful practice that was inexplicably not applied to the books of the prophets.

The Revised Bible, prepared nearly three hundred years after the King James Bible, remains that Bible's only officially recognized and authorized revision. Even so, it did not offer readers a translation in contemporary English, and although it was widely hailed and used for many years by specialists, neither the

American nor the English version was able to replace the King James Bible in the hearts of the general reader.

While the Revised Bible and the American Standard Version were not popular successes, they marked a turning point in Bible translation. From this point on scholars would no longer be reluctant out of deference to the venerable King James Bible to revise – or translate anew – the Bible. The virtual monopoly of the King James Bible was now a thing of the past; the modern translation tradition had begun.

REVISED STANDARD VERSION

In the period after World War I, the International Council of Religious Education, an American Protestant organization, began to plan for an updated revision of the Bible. In 1928 the Council acquired the rights to the American Standard Version and set up the American Standard Bible Committee for the purpose of determining what type of revision of the American Standard Version would be appropriate. After two years, this committee reached the conclusion that retaining the King James Bible unchanged was not an option. Some members wanted to completely ignore the Revised Version and the American Standard Version, but a majority agreed to use the 1901 American Standard Version as the basic text to be revised thoroughly. For this reason the new version was to be called the Revised Standard Version. When the project was authorized in 1937, the stated purpose was that the project should

> embody the best results of modern scholarship as to the meaning of the Scriptures, and express this meaning in English diction which is designed for use in public and private worship and preserves those qualities which have given to the King James version a supreme place in English literature.

Funds were short, however, due to the Great Depression, but in 1936 the council made a deal with Thomas Nelson & Sons to fund the project in exchange for exclusive rights to publish for ten years. The council wanted the project to be international with Canadian and British participation, but World War II (1939 – 1945) made this logistically impossible. The suggestion arose again in 1946, but by then the committee work was well under way and the British had decided to prepare a radically new translation of their own which would not be a revision of the King James Bible or the Revised Version.

The Revised Standard Version of the New Testament was published in 1946. The Old Testament was completed in 1951, and 1952 saw the release of the Bible. The title page notes the history:

THE HOLY BIBLE

Revised Standard Version
containing the Old and New Testaments
translated from the original tongues
being the Version set forth A.D. 1611
revised A.D. 1881 – 1885 and A.D. 1901
compared with the most ancient authorities
and revised A.D. 1946 – 1952
Thomas Nelson & Sons
New York, Toronto, Edinburgh

This was therefore a revision of a revision. Of course, since the King James Bible purported to be a revision of the Bishops' Bible, itself based on Tyndale, the revisions go back at least four layers.

RESPONSE TO THE REVISED STANDARD VERSION

Almost all American Protestants were eager for this new revision. The unprecedented first printing of 900,000 copies quickly sold out; within ten years more than twelve million copies had been sold. But American fundamentalists reacted strongly against the new Bible. It appeared at a time when the demagogue Senator from Wisconsin, Joseph McCarthy (1908 – 1957), was fueling fears of Communists in the era of tension between the Western powers and the Soviet Union. He alleged that some of the Revised Standard Version revisers were Communists or "fellow travelers." These accusations were totally groundless, but the charges were not laid to rest until after McCarthy's death.

Fundamentalism is a movement that arose in the first decade of the twentieth century. The term is derived from a twelve-volume collection of essays by conservative Christians called "The Fundamentals: A Testimony to the Truth," published between 1910 and 1915. The purpose was to reaffirm orthodox Protestant beliefs such as belief in the inerrancy of the Scriptures, the virgin birth of Jesus and his bodily resurrection, and to zealously defend these beliefs against liberal theology, higher criticism of the Bible, and Darwinism and other beliefs that were viewed as harmful to Christianity. Fellow travelers was a term used for someone who was thought to be a Communist sympathizer although not a member of the Communist Party.

McCarthy's charges gave impetus to the opposition of many Protestant fundamentalists who already believed that the National Council of Churches was too liberal on social justice issues and theology. The publication of the Revised Standard Version provided an immediate occasion for them to engage in hostile action as this version had rendered several verses in ways they felt undercut the inerrant truth of the Bible. For example, in Isaiah 7.14, the Hebrew word *almah*, "young woman," had been translated in Greek by the Septuagint translators as *parthenos* which means "virgin." (Hebrew has a word that does mean "virgin," *betulah*, but this was not the word used in Isaiah.) Consequently, the writer of the Gospel of Matthew had used *parthenos* when citing Isaiah, thereby affirming that the Isaiah passage had foretold the virgin birth of Jesus. The King James translators had used "virgin" in the Isaiah passage, but the Revised Standard Version had adhered to the Hebrew "young woman." As Matthew had, evangelical and fundamentalist Christians understood the Isaiah verse to be looking forward to the virgin birth of Jesus; not using "virgin" in the Isaiah passage was deemed a denial of the virgin birth of Jesus.

Another example of a passage that was an issue for the fundamentalists is found in footnotes in Genesis 1.1 and 1.2. The Revised Standard Version offered "When God began to create" and "wind" as alternatives to "In the beginning God created" and "the Spirit."

Some fundamentalist critics also believed that at several points in the Old Testament the translation reflected the 1917 translation of the Jewish Publication Society of America. This was due, they suggested, to the inclusion of a Jewish scholar on the committee, Harry Orlinsky (1908 – 1992). One pastor in North Carolina burned copies of the new Bible, although apparently this had the effect of leading many people going out to buy it.

Apocrypha

The Episcopal Church in the United States requested the Apocrypha in the Revised Standard Version, and this was added to the translation in 1957. Since there was no American Standard Version of the Apocrypha, the Revised Standard Version Apocrypha was a revision of the Revised Version Apocrypha of 1894, as well as of the King James Version. To make the Bible more acceptable to Eastern Orthodox congregations, an expanded edition of the Apocrypha containing 3 and 4 Maccabees and Psalm 151 was released in 1977.

Roman Catholics had traditionally used the Douai-Reims Bible (1609 – 1610) a Latin-based English translation that predates the King James Bible as well as other Roman Catholic translations.

However, in 1965, the Catholic Biblical Association adapted the Revised Standard Version for Catholic use. The Revised Standard Version Catholic New Testament was published in 1965 and the full Bible in 1966. The books of the Apocrypha are interspersed throughout the Old Testament in the traditional order of the Vulgate.

NEW REVISED STANDARD VERSION

The Dead Sea Scrolls are a collection of about 900 documents, including texts of the Hebrew Bible, which were discovered between 1947 and 1956 in eleven caves in and around the ruins of the ancient settlement Khirbet Qumran on the northwest shore of the Dead Sea. They are in Hebrew, Aramaic and Greek, most of them on parchment, although some are on papyrus. They date from about 150 BCE to 70 CE. The texts are of great religious and historical significance, as they include the oldest known surviving copies of biblical and extra-biblical documents. These materials gave new insight into many places where the available Hebrew texts of some books of the Old Testament were unclear.

The Old Testament books of the Revised Standard Version were completed before the Dead Sea Scroll materials were widely available to scholars. But the Division of Christian Education (now Bible Translation and Utilization) of the National Council of Churches of the Churches of Christ in the United States, the copyright holder, recognized that these findings needed to be incorporated into the Bible.

Concerns about the archaic usage led some readers of the Revised Standard Version to advocate for further revision. The Revised Standard Version had retained a number of language forms that by the 1980s were completely out of date such as "thee" and "thou" when God was being addressed, although these had been dropped elsewhere. Further, many churches had become increasingly concerned about the way the male biased language of the Bible subtly promoted sexism and alienated female listeners when read in church. An example is "brothers" in contexts where a group that included men and women was being referred to or addressed. "Brothers and sisters" would be a better solution. The churches needed a translation that contained less masculine-orientated language wherever possible.

These issues led the National Council of Churches to establish a project to revise the Revised Standard Version. Called the New Revised Standard Version, it was published in 1989. Although the language is now much clearer than that of the Revised Standard Version, and although its attention to issues of gender language was extremely important to the contemporary churches, this revision still reflects the King James Bible and is clearly a formal equivalence type of translation.

Formal equivalence and dynamic equivalence as approaches to translation will be discussed later in this chapter.

There are three editions of the New Revised Standard Version. One contains the sixty-six books of the Old and New Testament that most Protestants consider canonical. A second edition contains the Apocrypha placed before the New Testament. Many Episcopal and Lutheran Churches use this edition. A third edition, designed for use by Roman Catholic readers, included the Apocrypha books, but presented them in the order that they were in the Latin Vulgate Bible.

CRITICISM OF THE NEW REVISED STANDARD VERSION

Many of the criticisms of this revision were similar to those aimed at the Revised Standard Version. It was for many conservative Protestants too liberal as it continued to render *almah* as "young woman" in Isaiah 7.14, as well as other verses they considered to be in error. In addition, because the New Revised Standard Version frequently departs from a literal translation of the text in favor of gender neutrality, critics argue it departed from the heritage of preserving the literal text of Scripture that was the distinguishing feature of translations in the Tyndale/King James tradition.

The Orthodox Churches agreed with many of these criticisms despite the fact Orthodox scholars had participated in the revision. The main problem for these churches, however, was that they continued to use the Septuagint Greek text of the Old Testament as the translation base, not original language Hebrew. In 1990 the Orthodox Church in America decided not to permit the use of the New Revised Standard Version in liturgy or Bible studies.

NEW INTERNATIONAL VERSION

As already noted, many evangelical Christians objected to a number of renderings of the Revised Standard Version. A key issue was how to translate several Old Testament passages which they understood to be references to Jesus or his birth. For example, in Isaiah 7.14 as discussed earlier, as well as in a number of other passages, the Revised Standard Version revisers had translated the Old Testament first and foremost according to the Hebrew text and context. Respecting the integrity of the Old Testament, they did not attempt to translate it in light of New Testament theology.

As an evangelical response to the Revised Standard Version, the New International Version project was started after a meeting in 1965 at Trinity Christian College in Palos Heights, Illinois, between the Christian Reformed Church, the National Association of Evangelicals, and a group of conservative international scholars. Their express desire was to have a Bible in modern English that preserved traditional evangelical theology. The New York Bible Society, which later became the International Bible Society and is now known as Biblica, was selected to prepare the translation. The New Testament was released in 1973 and the full Bible in 1978. It underwent a minor revision in 1984. A major revision and update was announced on September 1, 2009 and was due out in 2011. Used primarily by evangelical Christians, it became the largest selling translation released in the twentieth century.

The translators state in the preface that they were committed "to the authority and infallibility of the Bible as God's Word in written form." Their first concern was "the accuracy of the translation and its fidelity to the thought of the biblical writers." Ironically, this conviction led them to smooth out several perceived biblical contradictions. For example, they added *your* into Matthew 13.32, so it becomes "Though it [the mustard seed] is the smallest of all *your* seeds," an apparent correction of a botanical error spoken by Jesus. In Genesis 2.17, the King James Bible accurately reflects the Hebrew text when God tells the man and the woman that if they ate of the tree of the knowledge of good and evil that they would die "on that day." The serpent contradicts this when talking to the woman, saying she won't die on that day. She and the man do eat, and they do not die, thereby making God's word unreliable and the serpent the one who told the truth. The New International Version eliminated this perception of God by translating "on that day" as "surely."

Despite the fact that the goal was to prepare a new translation in modern English, the New International Version is a revision. Very little of it is new. The translators drew on several mid-twentieth century translations: the New English Bible, the Jerusalem Bible, and the New Jewish Version, but primarily on the Revised Standard Version. Further, although for the most part it is less literal than the Revised Standard Version, in many places it is still very literal. Examples of expressions that readers might not understand include "Daughter of Tarshish" and "Virgin Daughter of Sidon" in Isaiah 23.10 and 23.12 referring to the people in the colonies of Spain in the first case and the city of Sidon in the second. "Anointing you with the oil of joy" in Psalm 45.7 is not modern English, and nor is "the first fruits of all their manhood" in Psalm 105.36. The end result is a Bible that is significantly close to the predecessor its revisers had so criticized.

New King James Version

In 1975 a number of conservative Baptist and Presbyterian ministers and scholars met to consider and organize a new revision of the King James Bible. The aim was to update the vocabulary and grammar of the King James Bible while preserving the classic style and beauty of the 1611 version. To a significant degree, the revisers followed the same Greek and Hebrew texts that the King James translators had. The task of updating the English of the King James Bible involved significant changes in word order, grammar, vocabulary, and spelling. One of the most significant features of this translation was its abandonment of the historic second person pronouns "thou", "thee", "ye", "thy", and "thine." The translators also modernized verb forms, for example changing "speaketh" to "speaks."

The Bible was published in 1982 by Thomas Nelson, Inc., the conservative protestant publisher who funded its development. It has met with criticism from two different directions. Most scholars point out that there are now many much older and more accurate Greek texts of the New Testament than the Textus Receptus that the King James translators had used. But that choice was deliberate as the revisers supported the position that only the Textus Receptus was inspired. Meanwhile, many others who believe that the King James Bible is the only translation that truly was inspired do not use this translation because it makes too many significant changes from the text it claims to honor. Despite these criticisms, this revision has found a niche in those churches who find this a helpful bridge between the original King James Bible and more modern syntax

A New Approach to Translation

The King James translators aimed at crafting a translation that was as accurate as they could make it and yet be in clear language that their readers would be able to understand. But they were also committed to staying as close as possible to the biblical form. They looked for vocabulary and sentence structures in English that were equivalent to what they saw in the Hebrew and Greek texts. While rarely word-for-word, this approach to translation, known as "formal equivalence," places the emphasis on the original word order, idiom and grammar of the text, even at the expense of more natural word order or expressions in the receptor language.

In the middle and later part of the twentieth century, a new approach was proposed and taught to translators in languages around the world. Called "dynamic equivalence" or "functional equivalence," this approach aimed at conveying the thought and meaning conveyed in the source texts, ignoring the original syntax and word order when adhering to them might obscure the meaning of the text. The aim was to produce translations that were the closest natural equivalent. In other words, translators were looking for equivalence in meaning to be expressed in the natural idiom of the target language while staying as close to the form of the original languages as this allowed them. Despite these differences in focus, in reality there is no sharp boundary between the two approaches; they represent different points on a continuum of translation approaches. Readers who are interested in comparing the two approaches should look at the examples at the end of this chapter.

The concept of dynamic or functional equivalence applied to Bible translation was developed by the American Bible Society linguist Dr. Eugene A. Nida (1914 – 2011). He also taught the procedures and methods that would ensure that the resulting translation reflected accurately the sense of the biblical texts. As a result of Nida's leadership, it was the American Bible Society that produced the first major translation in English that systematically followed the principles of dynamic equivalence, the Good News Bible, also known as Today's English Version. The New Testament was published in 1966 and the entire Bible ten years later. The American Bible Society prepared this translation specifically for non-native speakers of English, but because the translation communicated the biblical text so clearly, it has been extremely popular in North America and Great Britain and with

English speakers everywhere. By 1998 worldwide distribution was well over 225 million.

A number of other translations followed similar principles to some degree. These include the New Jerusalem Bible, the Revised English Bible, the New Living Translation, the New Century Version, the Contemporary English Version, and God's Word Translation.

A dynamic equivalent translation is not the same as a paraphrase. By calling for a translation that is "the closest natural equivalent," the method insists on moving away from the form of the original only when it is necessary to do so to be natural in the target language, and even then the translator should be close to the original if possible, or at least not to contradict it. An example would be in 1 Corinthians 16.20 where the King James Bible has "All the brethren greet you" The Message, a paraphrase, has "All the friends here say hello." The Good News Translation, following dynamic equivalence, has "All the believers here send greetings."

NEW ENGLISH BIBLE AND REVISED ENGLISH BIBLE

Near the time when the copyright to the English Revised Version was due to expire (1935), the Oxford and Cambridge University presses, the copyright holders, began to look into whether or not there was a need to produce a revision in modern British English. The Church of Scotland, taking the lead, decided a completely new translation would be preferable. In 1946, the Church of Scotland and the Church of England, along with nine smaller British and Irish church bodies, organized such a project relying on British and European scholarship.

From 1950 on, the Welsh scholar C. H. Dodd (1884 – 1973), a Cambridge New Testament professor, led the project. The Bible, including the Apocrypha, was released in 1970 (the New Testament had come out in 1961). The translators had followed the principles of dynamic equivalence, but had used a high literary level of language in an attempt to emulate the King James Bible.

In the years following the release of the New English Bible, there were a number of advances in biblical and textual scholarship which many scholars realized needed to be incorporated in a revision. Also, many critics felt that some of the renderings in the translation reflected Dodd's idiosyncratic interpretations rather than mainstream scholarship. Although this translation was the work of a committee, the project did not have the safeguards built in as had the King James Bible project, with the result that one scholar, in this case Dodd, could exert undue influence. Further, the New English Bible had been prepared when there was little concern with the issue of gender bias in language. To remedy these problems, the churches in Britain and Ireland established a committee to revise the New English Bible under the leadership of Professor W. D. McHardy. The resulting revision, the Revised English Bible was published in 1989.

Like the New English Bible, the Revised English Bible has found its principal audience among the British educated public. Due to its high literary level, however, it never achieved great popular success.

English Standard Version

The English Standard Version is a translation that intentionally moved away from dynamic equivalence to formal equivalence. Although the New International Version was promoted as an evangelical translation, some well-known conservative Christian leaders did not accept the way it used gender-neutral language where the original texts allowed it. In 1977,

James Dobson, the founder and leader of Focus on the Family, an organization whose purpose is to strengthen what it considers traditional marriage and families, called a meeting of other like-minded leaders to resolve this issue. This group decided to prepare a revision of the Revised Standard Version. Their proposed revision would correct what they saw as non-Christian interpretations of the Revised Standard Version in the Old Testament and would improve the accuracy through more literal renderings.

The translators stated that their intent was to produce a readable and accurate translation that would stand in the tradition of Bible translations beginning with William Tyndale and culminating in the King James Version. In their own words, they aimed to follow a literal translation philosophy. To that end, they sought as far as possible to capture the precise wording of the original text and the personal style of each Bible writer, while taking into account differences of grammar, syntax, and idiom between current literary English and the original languages. Also in keeping with the tradition of the King James Bible, they included the Apocrypha even though most conservative Protestant churches do not consider these books Scripture.

The group sought and received permission from the National Council of Churches to use the 1971 edition of the Revised Standard Version as the English textual basis. Only about five to ten percent of the Revised Standard Version text was changed in the English Standard Version. Many of these changes were made to satisfy objections to some of the interpretations in the Revised Standard Version that conservative Protestants had considered as theologically liberal, for example, changing the translation of the Hebrew *almah* from "young woman" to "virgin" in Isaiah 7.14. The language was modernized to remove "thou" and "thee" and to replace obsolete words, for example "jug" for "cruse."

The result is a translation that is more literal than the New International Version, but more idiomatic than some other attempts at formal equivalence translation. It was published in 2001 by Crossways Bibles, a division of Good News Publishers.

Several evangelical denominations and churches have begun to use the translation. For example, the Lutheran Church Missouri-Synod adopted it as its official text. The publishers and promoters speak of this translation as the "Bible of the future," although this seems unlikely given its extremely archaic language and awkward sentences that are far from Standard English.

Ephesians 1.3 – 15 will give readers a sense of the English Standard Version:

3 Blessed be the God and Father of our Lord Jesus Christ, who has blessed us in Christ with every spiritual blessing in the heavenly places, 4 even as he chose us in him before the foundation of the world, that we should be holy and blameless before him. In love 5 he predestined us for adoption as sons through Jesus Christ, according to the purpose of his will, 6 to the praise of his glorious grace, with which he has blessed us in the Beloved. 7 In him we have redemption through his blood, the forgiveness of our trespasses, according to the riches of his grace, 8 which he lavished upon us, in all wisdom and insight 9 making known to us the mystery of his will, according to his purpose, which he set forth in Christ 10 as a plan for the fullness of time, to unite all things in him, things in heaven and things on earth.

11 In him we have obtained an inheritance, having been predestined according to the purpose of him who works all things according to the counsel of his will, 12 so that we who were the first to hope in Christ might be to the praise of his glory. 13 In him you also, when you heard the word of truth, the gospel of your salvation, and believed in him, were sealed with the promised Holy Spirit, 14 who is the guarantee of our inheritance until we acquire possession of it, to the praise of his glory.

JEWISH TRANSLATIONS

(The Jewish Bible includes only what Christians refer to as the Old Testament.)

In the eighteenth and nineteenth centuries Jewish communities in Europe and America began increasingly to study the Bible, a trend which led to the preparation of a number of translations. One of the first was a project initiated by Moses Mendelssohn (1729 – 1786) to prepare a Judeo-German translation. A French Bible was completed in 1851, and translations in Dutch, Hungarian, Russian and Yiddish followed.

Mendelssohn, a Jewish German philosopher, is known as the father of Reform Judaism. The composer Felix Mendelssohn was a descendant.

In 1789, Isaac Delgado, a Hebrew teacher in England, published an English translation of parts of the first five books of the Bible known as the Chumash or Torah. It was not a continuous text, but a series of revised passages. Taking the King James Bible as his base, he made three kinds of what he called corrections: (1) wherever the King James Bible deviates from the genuine sense of the Hebrew expressions; (2) where the King James Bible obscures the meaning of the text; (3) when the translation brings about what seems like a contradiction.

Several other Jewish scholars also published individual sections of text, all relying on the King James Bible as their base. The first translation of the whole Hebrew Bible was prepared by Abraham Benisch (1814 – 1878) in 1861, the *Jewish School and Family Bible.*

In America, the most important Jewish leader in the period before the Civil War was Isaac Leeser (1806 – 1868). His translation of the Bible published in 1853 was the first Jewish translation in English in the United States. Leeser reasoned that if the Bible was the center of American Christianity, then it should also be the center of American Judaism. And if that Christian Bible was the King James Bible, then it also had to be the basis of a Jewish version. His aim therefore was to prepare a translation that would not run counter to rabbinic understanding, but at the same time would essentially be a Judaizing of the King James Bible. For example, in 1 Samuel 3.3, the King James Bible has the young Samuel lying down "in the temple of the Lord," but Leeser's translation has Samuel "sleep in (the hall of) the temple." This insertion in parentheses brought the translation into agreement with the rabbinic understanding of priestly protocol. There are some other notable differences with the King James Bible: (1) his use of "s" for "spirit" in Genesis 1.2 and for "son" in Psalm 2.12 where the King James Bible has "S;" (2) *almah* in Isaiah 7.14 is rendered "this young woman."

TANAKH

In 1908, in the United States the Jewish Publication Society undertook to prepare a new Jewish Bible. Rather than revising Leeser, however, they chose to prepare a light revision of the Revised Version. The new Bible appeared in 1917. Some distinctive characteristics include printing all poetry in the form of poetry and capitalizing the "thees" and "thous" when they referred to the Deity.

This translation served the American Jewish community through much of the twentieth century, but by the middle of the century, many American Jews began to ask for a more intelligible translation that was based on the most recent scholarship. In 1953 the Jewish Publication Society undertook to prepare a new translation. Among their aims was that this translation retain as far as possible "the flavor of the King James Bible and the existing Jewish Publication Society version." However, the chief editor, Harry Orlinsky, who also served on the committee preparing the New Revised Standard Version, maintained that he did not refer to the King James Version when working on the *Tanakh*. Further, the translators followed the principles of dynamic equivalence and steered away from attempting a formal equivalence. It was finally published in 1985 under the title *Tanakh.*

Tanakh is a name used in Judaism for the books which make up the Jewish Bible. "Tanakh" is an acronym made up of the first letters in Hebrew of the three traditional subdivisions of the Bible: Torah ("teaching") refers to the first five books, Genesis through Deuteronomy; Nevi'im ("Prophets"); Ketuvim ("Writings"), hence *TaNaKh.*

DOUAI-RHEIMS BIBLE

Beginning with Wycliffe in the fourteenth century, the Roman Catholic Church opposed vernacular translations. A principal reason was that these translations were based on the original languages not on the Church's official translation, the Latin Vulgate. English-speaking Catholics needed a translation, but until the middle of the sixteenth century, the only translations that were available were Protestant, for example the Tyndale, Coverdale, Great, Geneva and Bishops' Bibles. During the six-teenth century, when they were being persecuted in England, a number of English Roman Catholic scholars took refuge in Douai in France, and later in Rheims. Some of them undertook to prepare a Roman Catholic translation that could be used by English-speaking Catholics, and could also be an aid to convert the English to Catholicism. The translation was based on the Latin Vulgate translation. The New Testament was published in 1582. The Old Testament was published in two stages in 1609 and 1610. Undoubtedly the King James translators would have had access to this translation, but they do not list it as one of the translations that they referred to.

The Douai-Rheims translation was not widely used by Catholics until the English bishop Richard Challoner (1691

– 1781) borrowed heavily from the King James Bible and revised the Douai-Rheims between 1749 and 1752. He was assisted by a Carmelite Francis Blyth (1705 – 1772). He modified the odd prose of the Douai-Rheims substantially so that in the end it bore little resemblance to the original, but that name was retained. The Challoner revision remained the Bible of the majority of English-speaking Catholics well into the twentieth century.

The Order of the Brothers of Our Lady of Mount Carmel or Carmelites is a Catholic religious order perhaps founded in the 12th century on Mount Carmel. The spiritual focus of the Carmelites is contemplative prayer.

The Douai-Rheims Bible was first published in America in 1790 by Mathew Carey of Philadelphia. Several American editions followed in the nineteenth and early twentieth centuries, including an edition published in 1899 by the John Murphy Company of Baltimore. In 1941 the New Testament and Psalms of the Douay-Rheims Bible were again heavily revised to produce the New Testament (and in some editions, the Psalms) of the Confraternity Bible. But the changes were so extensive that it was no longer identified as the Douay-Rheims.

The Confraternity Bible, or the Holy Bible, Confraternity Version, is a blanket title given to various English language Bible translation compilations which were periodically released by the Confraternity of Christian Doctrine starting in 1941 and culminating in, but not completely inclusive of, the release of the 1970 New American Bible. The Confraternity of Christian Doctrine is an organization founded in Rome in 1562 for the purpose of giving Christian education.

NEW AMERICAN BIBLE

Starting in 1948, the Confraternity of Christian Doctrine began to revise the Confraternity Bible on the basis of the original languages. Then the Second Vatican Council (1962 – 1965) instituted a number of liturgical reforms in the Catholic Church, including authorizing the use of vernacular languages in liturgy. Under these new guidelines, the Confraternity continued this project and published what was now called the New American Bible in 1970. It continues to go through a series of revisions, with the fourth edition released in 2011.

Pope John XXIII convened the council in 1962 with the goal of addressing a number of issues that faced the modern church including liturgy, mass communications and the role of bishops. One major decision was to permit and encourage using the vernacular languages in the mass instead of Latin, and encouraging translations of the Bible in vernacular languages that were based on the Greek and Hebrew texts, not on the Latin.

JERUSALEM BIBLE AND NEW JERUSALEM BIBLE

The most important development in modern Roman Catholic Bible translation came by way of French scholarship. In 1948, the Dominican École Biblique in Jerusalem began to publish commentaries and French translation on each book of the Bible. (The Dominicans are also known as the Order of Preachers. This Catholic order was founded in the fifteenth century.) Father Roland de Vaux (1903 – 1971) led a team of first-class scholars. The Bible, known as the Bible de Jérusalem, appeared in 1956. English scholars immediately recognized the high quality of the work, and so a team began to prepare an English version. The

Jerusalem Bible was published in 1966. The translation was influenced by the French translation to the degree that most scholars suggest it was essentially a translation of the French. The committee denied this. It was the first widely accepted Roman Catholic English translation since the Douai-Rheims. (One of the contributors was the Oxford professor J.R.R. Tolkien, best known for his novels *The Hobbit* and *The Lord of the Rings* trilogy. He translated Jonah.)

In 1985 a completely updated version, the New Jerusalem Bible, was published. This edition was based entirely on the original languages. It is in some ways more a formal equivalent type of translation than was the Jerusalem Bible, although it has used more gender-inclusive language. But the notes are retained, making this one of the best study Bibles available.

TRANSLATIONS BY INDIVIDUALS

Several translations prepared by individuals have also been widely used. Most of these lie outside the King James Bible revision tradition.

The Scottish New Testament teacher and minister James Moffat (1870 – 1944), for example, decided to prepare a translation in plain English. The New Testament was published in 1913, and the Old in 1926. Most readers did find his translation easy to read, but were often startled at some of the other changes he made. For example, he believed the first five books of the Old Testament had been written by four different authors, and he used different typefaces for each of the authors to show this. The traditional view of most fundamentalist Christians and Jews was that Moses had written all five books. Moffat also rearranged the order of the biblical texts to reflect his judgment about the content, authorship and historicity. For example, John 14 comes after John 15 and 16 in his Bible.

Despite the fact that many people objected to these changes, his translation proved popular and it was a forerunner of many paraphrased versions in later years.

Edgar J. Goodspeed (1871 – 1962) was an American liberal scholar and Greek New Testament scholar who taught for many years at the University of Chicago. He was the New Testament translator of An American Translation, a Bible that was published in 1949. The Old Testament was prepared by a committee of scholars led by J.M. Powis Smith. Their goal was to produce a translation in contemporary English that reflected modern scholarship. Because of his detailed scholarship and gift for using idiomatic English, Goodspeed's New Testament is considered one of the premier American translations.

J.B. Phillips (1906 – 1982), an English clergyman was distressed that the children and young people in the parish in London he was serving during World War II did not understand the King James Bible. In the periods when he was in the bomb shelters during the London Blitz, Phillips began to paraphrase the Epistle to the Colossians. He found the youth were drawn to his version because they could finally understand what the Bible was saying. He continued the work after the war, publishing individual sections as he finished them, and the whole New Testament appeared in 1958. Phillips became one of Britain's best-known Bible communicators. He attempted to translate the Old Testament, but after releasing parts of the Prophets, he abandoned the project. Phillips presented the biblical materials in a fresh and creative way which gave his readers new access to the Scriptures.

The Blitz was the sustained bombing of Britain by Nazi Germany between 7 September 1940 and 10 May 1941, in the Second World War. While the Blitz hit many towns and cities across the country, it began with the bombing of London for fifty-seven consecutive night. By the end of May 1941, over 43,000 civilians, half of them in London, had been killed by bombing and more than a million houses were destroyed or damaged in London alone.

Here is a sample of how Phillips was able to make even a theological passage of Colossians, 2.16-19, come alive:

In view of these tremendous facts, don't let anyone worry you by criticizing what you eat or drink, or what holy days you ought to observe, or bothering you over new moons or Sabbaths. All these things have at most only a symbolical value; the solid fact is Christ. Nor let any man cheat you of your joy in Christ by persuading you to make yourselves "humble" and fall down and worship angels. Such a man, inflated by an unspiritual imagination, is pushing his way into matters he knows nothing about, and in his cleverness forgetting the head. It is from the head alone that the body, by natural channels, is nourished and built up and grows according to God's laws of growth.

MANY OTHER NEW TRANSLATIONS

Since 1800, Bible translation has been a growth industry. In most languages readers have only two or three translations to choose from, or even just one, while speakers of English are offered new translations almost yearly. The general acceptance of dynamic equivalent translation principles is one key reason for this growth. The relative wealth of English-speaking countries is another. It is possible today to virtually custom-fit a translation to any theological, literary, and sociological preference – provided a funder can be found. Finding a translation that best meets your needs can be a challenge.

The twentieth century saw scores of new translations of the Bible. In addition to those already described, some of the other well-known translations are the New Century Version, the New Living Translation, the Complete Jewish Bible, the Contemporary English Version and The Message. Readers often want to know how to evaluate the many revisions and translations that are available. There are at least these criteria:

1. What Hebrew and Greek texts did they follow? Most Bible readers want a translation that was based on the best texts available. Apart from the King James Bible which appeared before the modern era of textual scholarship, and the New King James Bible which insists on using the same base texts as the original King James Bible, newer revisions and translations have taken advantage of modern textual scholarship.

2. Is the translation accurate? All translators find that their theological stance affects how they translate to some degree. It cannot be avoided. Some inaccurate or minority renderings are more deliberate, however. The New World Translation of the Jehovah's Witnesses, a group that does not believe in the divinity of Christ, has "the Word was a god" in John 1.1; most translations have rendered the Greek as "the Word was God." Most translators, however, try to reflect the mainstream of contemporary biblical scholarship.

3. Is the translation easy to understand? Revisions of the King James Bible or even revisions of revisions rarely produce clear, natural English. Those translations that have focused on the meaning of the text rather than on the form of the original language tend to be in more natural English.

A READER'S GUIDE

As a guide for examining translations, readers are invited to use these three criteria to compare translations much as in the evaluations below of Hebrews 1.1-3 in several rather different versions.

KING JAMES VERSION

God, who at sundry times and in divers manners spake in time past unto the fathers by the prophets,
²Hath in these last days spoken unto us by his Son, whom he hath appointed heir of all things, by whom also he made the worlds;
³Who being the brightness of his glory, and the express image of his person, and upholding all things by the word of his power, when he had by himself purged our sins, sat down on the right hand of the Majesty on high.

NEW REVISED STANDARD VERSION

Long ago God spoke to our ancestors in many and various ways by the prophets, ²but in these last days he has spoken to us by a Son, whom he appointed heir of all things, through whom he also created the worlds. ³He is the reflection of God's glory and the exact imprint of God's very being, and he sustains all things by his powerful word. When he had made purification for sins, he sat down at the right hand of the Majesty on high.

NEW INTERNATIONAL VERSION

In the past God spoke to our forefathers through the prophets at many times and in various ways, ²but in these last days he has spoken to us by his Son, whom he appointed heir of all things, and through whom he made the universe. ³The Son is the radiance of God's glory and the exact representation of his being, sustaining all things by his powerful word. After he had provided purification for sins, he sat down at the right hand of the Majesty in heaven.

NEW JERUSALEM BIBLE

At many moments in the past and by many means, God spoke to our ancestors through the prophets; but ²in our time, the final days, he has spoken to us in the person of his Son, whom he appointed heir of all things and through whom he made the ages. *³He is the reflection of God's glory and bears the impress of God's own being, sustaining all things by his powerful command; and now that he has purged sins away, he has taken his seat at the right hand of the divine Majesty on high.*

GOOD NEWS BIBLE

In the past God spoke to our ancestors many times and in many ways through the prophets, ²but in these last days he has spoken to us through his Son. He is the one through whom God created the universe, the one whom God has chosen to possess all things at the end. ³He reflects the brightness of God's glory and is the exact likeness of God's own being, sustaining the universe with his powerful word. After achieving forgiveness for the sins of all human beings, he sat down in heaven at the right side of God, the Supreme Power.

REVISED ENGLISH BIBLE

When in times past God spoke to our forefathers, he spoke in many and varied ways through the prophets. ²But in this the final age he has spoken to us in his Son, whom he has appointed heir of all things; and through him he created the universe. ³He is the radiance of God's glory, the stamp of God's very being, and he sustains the universe by his word of power. When he had brought about purification from sins, he took his seat at the right hand of God's Majesty on high.

CONTEMPORARY ENGLISH VERSION

Long ago in many ways and at many times God's prophets spoke his message to our ancestors. ²But now at last God sent his Son to bring his message to us. God created the universe by his Son, and everything will someday belong to the Son. ³God's Son has all the brightness of God's own glory and is like him in every way. By his own mighty word he holds the universe together. After the Son had washed away our sins, he sat down at the right side of the glorious God in heaven.

<u>NEW CENTURY VERSION</u>

In the past God spoke to our ancestors through the prophets many times and in many different ways. ²But now in these last days God has spoken to us through his Son. God has chosen his Son to own all things, and through him he made the world. ³The Son reflects the glory of God and shows exactly what God is like. He holds everything together with his powerful word. When the Son made people clean from their sins, he sat down at the right side of God, the Great One in heaven.

<u>THE MESSAGE</u>

(The Message is usually considered a paraphrase rather than a true translation. But the translator, Eugene Peterson, has attempted to express the meaning of the biblical text in contemporary, common language, and it is worth examining his work using the same criteria of text, accuracy and clarity.)

Going through a long line of prophets, God has been addressing our ancestors in different ways for centuries. Recently he spoke to us directly through his Son. By his Son, God created the world in the beginning, and it will all belong to the Son at the end. This son perfectly mirrors God, and is stamped with God's nature. He holds everything together by what he says – powerful words!

After he finished the sacrifice for sins, the Son took his honored place high in the heavens right alongside God, far higher than any angel in rank and rule.

OBSERVATIONS

- In verse 2, what does "in these last days" of several versions mean? "Recently" or "the end of time"? The Contemporary English Version has "at last;" the Revised English Bible has "in this the final age," surely a high level of language; the New Jerusalem Bible covers both senses, "in our time, the final days."

- "Fathers" in verse 1 of the King James Bible has become "ancestors" in many other versions, eliminating the gender bias. But the New International Version retains the masculine with "forefathers."

- "by his son" of the King James Bible in verse 2 is "through" in Good News Bible and The Message, much better English.

- In verse 3 of the King James Bible, God has "purged our sins."The New International Version makes this general, "purification for sins," but the level of language is high. Good News Bible makes it clear whose sins are involved: "forgiveness for the sins of all human beings."

- "heir of all things" in verse 2 of the King James Bible may not mean much to contemporary readers. The Contemporary English Version, the Message and the Good News Bible make the meaning clear.

- What does "brightness of his glory" in verse 3 of the King James Bible or "radiance of God's glory" in the New International Version mean? "Reflects the brightness of God's glory" as in the New Century Version or the New Jerusalem Bible, while still not totally understandable, seems to help readers get a better understanding of the phrase.

- "The express image of his person" in verse 3 is very clear in the New Century Version: "shows exactly what God is like."

- In verse 2, the New Revised Standard Version has translated the Greek literally with "a son," which contrasts with "the prophets." But most other translations have followed the King James translators with "his Son," making the reference to Jesus explicit. There is no "his" in the Greek, which has literally "in a son."

The King James Bible was the standard Bible of the English speaking world for more than two hundred years, and even when newer translations appeared, readers continued to hold it in esteem. It had many short-comings and suffers from the inevitable changes in the English language. The translators used the best texts that were available to them, and were careful to render them accurately and in clear English. The nature of printing in the seventeenth century resulted in many misprints and errors. Today translators have access to much older and more accurate texts of both the Old and New Testaments. Although changes to the English language have made the text inaccessible to many modern readers, the King James Bible remains unchallenged for the beauty of its poetry and its influence on the language of generations. And as the examples above show, it continues to shape the language of English translations nearly four hundred years later.

THE KING JAMES
BIBLE TODAY

"After the seventeenth century the language and the specific texts of the Bible made themselves felt throughout American culture to an extent that visibly exceeded what was observable in the changing cultural situation in England." (Robert Alter. *Pen of Iron.* 2010. Page 180.)

For a period of at least three centuries, in North America and to a lesser degree in Britain, familiarity with the Scriptures was a significant part of the culture. Many of the founders of the American colonies went to the New World out of deeply religious motives, and much of the society they established was based on ideologies and principles they discovered in their Bible. People in America read the Bible daily and heard it from the pulpit. Their daily speech was filled with biblical quotes and references to the degree that they may not even have been aware of how much they were quoting the Bible. National leaders such as Thomas Jefferson, Abraham Lincoln and Woodrow Wilson could quote or refer to the Bible freely and expect their audiences to understand them. Writers drew on the Bible for their themes, allusions and idiom. The language and culture were suffused with knowledge of the Bible.

The Bible that they all quoted was the King James Bible. It was essentially the only Bible people knew. This is no longer the case. No English-speaking culture in the world is pervaded by Scripture as they once were for such a long period. For many, the Bible is simply not as relevant or as valued as it was just a few generations ago. Biblical illiteracy, that is, lack of knowledge of the Bible, is rampant. Furthermore, those who do read the Bible and value it are likely now to use a translation in more contemporary and understandable language than the King James Bible offers. Whereas the three hundredth anniversary of the King James Bible was a cause for widespread public celebration in 1911, the four hundredth is more likely to be marked by isolated academic convocations than by general celebration.

But yet the King James Bible's influence endures. It endures notably in the entertainment media and in several artistic domains, and it continues to be a key part of the African American church.

"When I want to know what something means, I turn to a translation that has expressed the meaning of a text in clear, natural English. But when I want to be drawn into a spiritual experience, then I read the King James Bible. It sounds religious. The fact it is slightly mysterious helps me feel somehow closer to God." – Quote from a highly educated and theologically sophisticated church woman

---

FILM AND STAGE

The King James Bible still is widely quoted in the movies. When Hollywood or evangelistic organizations make films based on biblical stories, almost inevitably the dialogue is either taken directly from the King James Bible or in language that sounds like the King James Bible. Makers of these films know that their audiences will not take their movies seriously if they don't sound "biblical," specifically, they have to sound like the King James Bible. For example, a key point in the plot of Krzysztof Kie lowski's 1993 film *Three Colors Blue* turned on 1 Corinthians 13 sung in Greek. The English version used the King James Bible. Or listen to the actor Richard Gere as David in Bruce Beresford's 1985 film *King David.* Much of the dialogue sounds like the King James Bible, although the film does not actually quote it.

The many films on the ministry, life, and suffering of Christ or Old Testament epics such as *The Ten Commandments* all show enormous influence of the King James Bible in the dialogue. The 1965 film *The Greatest Story Ever Told,* for example, opens with the narrator reading the prologue to the Gospel of John in the King James Bible, and much of the dialogue in the movie is either taken from the King James Bible or uses verb forms and structures that echo it.

The King James Bible has often been heard on stage. In 1978 the British actor Alex McCowen filled a London theater night after night performing the Gospel of Mark. He then took the performance to New York City and Broadway audiences responded equally enthusiastically. The musical play *Godspell,* first produced in New York in 1971, is another example. This is a play with very modern popular music and dance, but dialogue adapted from the Gospel of Matthew in the King James Version, often presented playfully and with humor. One might think that the King James Bible would be incompatible with rock music, but the writers knew that only if the script sounded like the King James Bible would people take the references seriously.

Godspell is an old spelling of "Gospel." During the play's initial run on London's West End, the British and Foreign Bible Society printed an edition of the Gospel of Matthew with the distinctive design of the playbill on the cover. As theater goers left the performance, they were met by BFBS volunteers distributing the booklet: "You've seen the play, now get the book," they called out.

A recent example of a graphic novel bears out the same point. Robert Crumb (born 1943) is known for illustrating extended comic books for adults. Crumb's graphic novels usually tell stories that are socially critical and even subversive. Their themes are sometimes very dark. Crumb's illustrations, often graphically violent or sexual, are more important than the narrative text as it is these drawings that create the tone and atmosphere of the story.

Recently he turned his attention to the Bible. *The Book of Genesis Illustrated,* published in 2009, is not simply a comic book version of Genesis. Crumb interprets the story through his art as it graphically portrays human bodies, violence and sexual behavior. He argues that he has reproduced or translated every word of Genesis either through the illustrations or the dialogue. And for that he has turned to several translations, including the King James Bible and the translation of the first five books of the Bible by the literary critic Robert Alter.

Alter's translation, *The Five Books of Moses* was published in 2004. His purpose was to prepare a translation that represented accurately the "semantic nuances and the lively orchestration of literary effects of the Hebrew and at the same time has stylistic rhythmic integrity as literary English" (page xvi). Critical of modern translations, and even of the King James Bible, Alter nevertheless states that the King James Bible "remains the closest approach for English readers to the original – despite its frequent and at times embarrassing inaccuracies, despite its archaisms, and despite its insistent substitution of Renaissance English tonalities and rhythms for biblical ones" (p. xvii).

At key points, Crumb responds to the pull of the King James Bible for idioms and phrases to give his text gravitas. For example, Genesis 1.26 in the King James Bible reads

And God said, "Let us make man in our image, after our likeness: and let them have dominion over the fish of the sea, and over the fowl of the air, and over the cattle, and over all the earth, and over every creeping thing that creepeth upon the earth.

Crumb's version is

And God said, "Let Us make man in Our own image, after Our likeness; and let them have dominion over the fish of the sea and over the birds of the heavens, and the cattle, and over the earth, and over every crawling thing that crawls upon the earth.

Although some words are more modern, for example "birds" for "fowl" and "crawls" for "creepeth," the rhythm and idiom of "fish of the sea" and "birds of the heavens" from the King James have been retained.

Shouldn't a writer of a modern comic, a graphic novel, use contemporary English to accompany such a contemporary narrative form? Not at all. Crumb knew his book had to sound like the Bible that people knew.

THE AFRICAN AMERICAN CHURCH

Although many conservative Christian churches still use the King James Bible for preaching and personal study, this continued use is especially notable in the African American churches. For generations of African Americans, this Bible has been cherished as a source of comfort, inspiration, empowerment, and prophetic insights. Its language permeates the prayers, hymns and sermons to a much greater degree than in churches where the majority is of European descent. It also is visible in the art and literature of the community. The roots of this lie in the history of African Americans in this country. As slaves, and even during the decades of oppression that followed emancipation, African Americans turned to the Bible for a message of hope and of liberation. Their music, preaching and prayers were suffused with the Old Testament stories of the Exodus and the promise of new life in the Kingdom of Heaven. When they reached "over Jordan," there would be comfort and joy. That history is still fresh; it lingers in the memories of every new generations. Those words of comfort and hope are all drawn from or shaped by the King James Bible.

"While standing at an airport gate waiting to board a plane, I had the harrowing experience of being informed by cell phone of my mother's sudden and unexpected death. Sitting in a crowded center seat for the five-hour flight from San Francisco to Washington, I clutched a compact-sized KJV Bible. Not once did I open it, so perhaps the version did not matter, but somehow I was comforted by it." Cheryl J. Sanders, professor of Christian Ethics at Howard University School of Divinity.

A Future

The New Testament scholar Bruce Metzger (1914 – 2007), chair of the committee for the New Revised Standard Version, observed that Bible translation has been undertaken by increasing numbers of scholars and interested groups in contemporary times. He suggested that with such a great variety of translations available it is hard to see anything new in Scripture. As translations of different sorts have been prepared for targeted groups of readers, translations have become less exalted, more matter of fact. The notion of transcendent truth in Scripture seems to have been lost. People turn elsewhere for deep, perhaps mystical, religious experiences. But for centuries, the King James Bible was the shared Scripture of faith communities. It was ever present on the hearts and lips of Christians and Jews throughout the English-speaking world.

Printed editions of the King James Bible have differences among them. There have been revisions and revisions of revisions. There are also completely new translations. And yet the King James Bible continues to influence the English language, the arts and culture, and Christian life around the world.

> "The appeal of the King James Bible lay in part in the harmony it achieved between the oral and aural, between speaking and hearing. It was dignified without being labored, devout without being sanctimonious, simple without being frivolous, restrained without being inhibiting, and elevated while remaining accessible."
> – Lamin Sanneh, Yale Divinity School.

Thus it is that for four centuries God's Spirit has spoken through this translation. Despite its flaws, despite its limited original purpose of providing a Bible to be read in the churches of that day, despite the changes in the Church and changes that the King James translators would never have dreamt of, readers and listeners have continued to hear God's word through it. As the translators said in the preface:

> There are many other things we could mention, gentle Reader, if we had not gone beyond the limits of a preface already. It remains to commend you to God, and to his gracious Spirit, which is able to build further than we can ask or think. He removes the scales from our eyes, the veil from our hearts, opening our minds so that we may understand his word, enlarging our hearts, and correcting our affections, so that we may love it above gold and silver, indeed, so that we may love it to the end.

Deo Gratias. Happy Birthday, King James Bible.

CPSIA information can be obtained at www.ICGtesting.com
Printed in the USA
LVOW130052021012

301056LV00004B/101/P